ARYO-SEMITIC SPEECH:

A STUDY

IN

LINGUISTIC ARCHAEOLOGY.

BY

JAMES FREDERICK M^CCURDY.

Wipf & Stock
PUBLISHERS
Eugene, Oregon

Wipf and Stock Publishers
199 W 8th Ave, Suite 3
Eugene, OR 97401

Aryo-Semitic Speech
A Study in Linguistic Archaeology
By McCurdy, James F.
ISBN: 1-59244-823-2
Publication date 8/26/2004
Previously published by Warren F. Draper, 1881

Inscribed

TO MY REVERED INSTRUCTOR AND FRIEND,

PROFESSOR WILLIAM HENRY GREEN.

PREFACE.

THE following work is substantially a reprint of articles contributed to the Bibliotheca Sacra, the last of them having appeared in January of the present year. Inasmuch as the ground taken up by it has been regarded by many influential scientists as properly closed to the practical worker, and an attempt to compare the Aryan and Semitic systems of language is often spoken of as mere dilettanteism, it seems necessary to say a few words by way of apology.

The investigation whose results are here presented has been carried on under the conviction that the field should not be abandoned until inquiry should be proved to be a search for the undiscoverable, or, in other words, until true scientific methods should be proved to be unavailing. If it appears that hitherto the full resources of science have not been called out, investigation would seem to be not only legitimate but necessary. The following considerations may be adduced as having controlled the purpose of the work:

(1) It is possible to compare the *forms* of the two systems better than has been done hitherto. Proto-Aryan forms, which are used on the one side of the equations, have been brought out of late years with ever-increasing definiteness and accuracy. A dictionary of Proto-Aryan roots, generally reliable for comparative purposes, not only may be, but has been, constructed, and the processes which are involved in its grand results are to be commended to the study of every trained and cautious etymologist. What the principles are which should lead to equally valid results in the search for Proto-Semitic roots cannot long be a matter of doubt; and a sound and sure Semitic morphology is certainly within reach. In Chapter IV. I have presented an outline of the

morphology of both Aryan and Semitic roots, drawn up without reference to any harmonizing of the two systems, either in their principles of structure or in individual forms. Criticism from competent judges upon these attempts is earnestly desired, especially upon the Semitic investigation which necessarily contains much more that is new than appears in the discussion of Aryan roots.

(2) In regard to the other element of language with which etymology is necessarily concerned, namely the *meanings* of the roots, I am of the firm conviction that there is such a thing as a science of meanings. Speaking more definitely, there is a possibility of showing a development, according to certain general laws, in the train of ideas represented by any given word whose history may be accurately traced. This is the same as saying that the comparative *usage* of words is not a matter of utter uncertainty. Schleicher is the only glottologist of eminence who has maintained the contrary opinion; and he was almost forced to hold it in consequence of his doctrine of the purely physical nature of language, which necessarily makes phonology and morphology the main departments of comparative philology. But it is hard to see how etymology can be more than a plaything if, in tracing the history of words, we are not guided by observed analogies of usage in the case of kindred ideas; and this implies the possibility of discovering empirical laws. The principles which I believe to have prevailed in the development of meanings are these: First, the stock of ideas in the possession of primitive men was small. Second, these ideas were of the most simple and primitive kind. Third, the main part of every language was built up from a small number of roots, the rest (whether few or many) having perished in the struggle for existence. Fourth, with the growth of civilization came the development of thought; but thought and language go hand in hand, and with new objects and ideas there came a development of meanings in words as well as the formation of new vocables. Fifth, this growing potency and versatility of language naturally followed the line of advancing civilization; if the same word, for example, means

to cut and to plough, the former meaning is the earlier. Sixth, most roots express general notions, but such conceptions at first related only to the world of sense and physical action; the metaphysical is always later than the physical meaning of any word. These principles relating to early language are very general in their application, and ought to be universally admitted. If their validity is granted, the true method of procedure in such an investigation as ours becomes evident. From the current roots in the two systems of speech we must select for comparison only those which expressed primarily the same simple notions. We have already seen that it is possible to reduce such roots to their Proto-Aryan and Proto-Semitic forms. If they agree both in their primary meanings and in their forms, the two conditions of sound etymology are satisfied. It should also be noted that in tracing the history of meanings in the case of any given root great help may be obtained from etymological analogies observed elsewhere; and such illustration has been sought as much as possible in the present work.

Two or three remarks may be made with reference to general objections urged against the admissibility of comparing linguistic systems whose structural principles differ. I confess that the only objection which seems worthy of the consideration of a linguistic philosopher is that based upon the assumption that language must have begun with sentences and not with single words, and that therefore the typical sentence form of each family must have distinguished it from all others from its earliest days. I even believe, with Steinthal, that human language, in its strict sense, only began with the use of the sentence, or the employment of a subject and predicate; but I also hold, with the same master, that the sentence form was not necessarily permanent. Nor did both of its parts necessarily consist of full-grown words. The theory that men first spoke in *roots* and the theory that they first spoke in *sentences* are both wrong or both right, according as they are understood by their advocates. This remark is made as preliminary to the discussion on p. 50 ff.

Objections from the side of ethnology or anthropology are

not entitled to much consideration. The fact is, that the main evidence for a distinction of Aryan and Semitic *races* is drawn from linguistic considerations. But that evidence is worthless because language does not necessarily differentiate races. There is, indeed, little evidence on either side from ethnology, and none at all from anthropology. If it should even appear certain that the Semites came from Northern Arabia and the Aryans from Central Asia, that would prove nothing except that reports have not reached us from any earlier *habitat*.

Attention should be called to the tentative character of the first division of Chapter III. The observations there made on pre-historic sounds are not offered in the way of complete scientific induction. They are only intended to show the possibility that the phonetic systems of the two families were originally the same. That branch of the discussion is not of such positive value as is claimed for the rest of the work. I should like to offer something better on the more obscure questions of comparative Semitic phonology; but the results of late researches in Germany do not seem to me to be more conclusive, and my own observations, written two years ago, are allowed to remain in the meanwhile. No question of form or meaning discussed in the book is affected by their correctness or falsity.

Finally it should be said that the *facts* brought out in this work are presented for the candid judgment of linguistic students rather than the conclusions arrived at. If it is *proved* that the Aryan and the Semite used the same sounds to express most of their essential primitive ideas the facts which make this certain become the permanent possession of science. How the linguistic philosopher as a psychologist or physiologist may account for the facts is, in the meantime, a matter of minor consideration.

J. F. McCURDY.

PRINCETON, N. J., April 21, 1881.

TABLE OF CONTENTS.

                                                          PAGE

CHAP. I.— PAST AND PRESENT TREATMENT OF THE SUBJECT, . . 1–22

Two main tests of linguistic relationship, 1. — The grammatical test surer than the etymological; prejudice against the latter, 2. — General principles to be borne in mind: all comparative linguistic reasoning is only of the *probable* kind; facts of science alone, and not current philosophizing, to be deferred to, 3–5. — Statement of the true method of procedure, 5.

History of opinion divided into two periods by the rise of comparative philology as a science, 5. — The pre-scientific tendency: Hebrew looked upon as the parent and primitive type of languages; occasion and value of this theory, 6, 7. — Examples of etymologizing which illustrated it, 8, 9 — The scientific era: two opposite and wrong tendencies since its inauguration, 10. — Instances of hasty generalizing: Adelung; Humboldt; Bopp, 11. — Kindred theory of affinity between Aryan, Semitic, and North-African families: Lepsius, Benfey, Bunsen, Schwartze, 11, 12. — Cautious views and tentative comparisons of Gesenius, 12, 13. — Untenable system of Fürst and Franz Delitzsch, 13–15. — Theories of Ewald, 15, 16. — "Wurzelwörterbuch" of Ernst Meier, 16. — Speculations of von Raumer and of Ascoli, 16–18. — Important essay of Friedrich Delitzsch criticised, 18–21. — Theory of J. Grill, 21. — Discordant views of other linguistic authorities, 22.

CHAP. II. — CRITERIA OF RELATIONSHIP, ... 23–52

Elements of language to be considered in comparing linguistic families, 23. — General remarks on the divergence in sounds, structural principles, and vocables between the Aryan and Semitic systems, 23–25. — Scheme of the treatment of the whole subject of the work, 25. — Comparison of sounds; phonology not a primary criterion of relationship; true aim and methods of phonological investigations, 26–28. — Comparison of structural peculiarities: conditions of the inquiry, 28, 29. — Attempt of Ewald to reconcile the divergencies in the placing of inflective elements, in the constitution of roots, in syntactical characteristics, 29–33. — Further remarks on the same subject; occasions of the diversity of the Aryan and Semitic sentence, 33, 34. — Meagre and unsatisfactory result of all these inquiries, 34–36.

Preliminaries to the comparison of single words: objection on general grounds to the admissibility of such processes; the objection not in the true spirit of science, 36–38. — Contention that the present types of speech

ix

TABLE OF CONTENTS.

necessarily rest on diversities of origin. Worthlessness of the ethnological argument, 38, 39. — The proper inferences to be drawn from the facts of dialectic variations, 40–42. — Objection that the structural peculiarities of linguistic types are original and permanent; arguments to show the possibility and probability of transitions, 42–45. — Illustrations from actual changes in language, 45, 46. — Analysis of elements in inflectional forms leads to the same conclusion, 46–49. — Objection on the ground of the greater complexity of ancient forms of expressions. Misconception of the real conditions of the case, 49, 50. — Objection that since language begins with sentences and not with words the sentence-form must have differentiated each family from the beginning. Fallacies involved in the argument, 50–52.

CHAP. III. — COMPARATIVE PHONOLOGY, ... 53–78

Questions comprised under this subject, 53. — The first task is to reduce the Aryan and Semitic alphabets to their primary limits. Main work to be done in the Semitic department, 53, 54. — The gutturals; their probable course of development and their mutual relations in the Semitic family, 54–60. — Comparison with the Aryan alphabet, 60. — History of v (w) and y in Aryan and Semitic, 60, 61. — Treatment of r and l, 61–63; m and n, 63, 64. — The sibilants, 64–68. — The mutes or explosives, 69–71. — Remarks on the vowels, 72. — Caution as to treatment of secondary sounds, 72.

Actual phonetic representation in Aryan and Semitic speech, and a tabular scheme, 72, 73. — Remarks on the peculiarities of the facts presented, 73, 74. — Notice of the objection that Aryo-Semitic roots, if they ever existed, would not probably have preserved their original sounds; Max Müller quoted and replied to, 74–77. — List of Proto-Aryan and Proto-Semitic consonants as a recapitulation, 78.

CHAP. IV. — MORPHOLOGY OF ROOTS, ... 79–116

Apparent confusion in processes of root-formation in both systems; need of showing the principles that have prevailed, 79, 80. — Definition of a true root, 80. — Apparently all roots are not primary; two-fold distinction to be made in roots, 80, 81. — Roots of the Aryan family; development of secondary roots by modification of old elements: 1. through weakening of a vowel; 2. through the strengthening or nasalizing of a vowel; 3. through transposition, 81–83. — Development through additional sounds: 1. the sounds prefixed, 83, 84; 2. the sound or sounds affixed; definition of "root-determinatives," 85. — Post-determinative a, 85; k, g, gh, 85, 86; t, d, dh, n, 86; p, bh, m, 86, 87; y, v, r (l), 87; s, 87. — Prepositions did not probably enter into the development of secondary roots, 87, 88. — Classification of results of investigation, 88. — Speculations as to the relative importance of so-called determinatives or secondary formatives, 88, 89. — The fuller forms are probably later than the simple roots, 89–91. — We cannot get at the signification of the determinatives; they are probably as primary as the simple roots, 91, 92. — Any true Proto-Aryan may be compared with any true Proto-Semitic root; criterion of a Proto-Aryan root, 92; criterion of a Proto-Semitic, 92, 93. — Remarkable peculiarity of

TABLE OF CONTENTS.

triliteralism in Semitic root-formation; a question arises as to its originality, 93, 94. — Arguments to show that *uniform* triliteralism is not original: evidence from various classes of "imperfect" verbs; three of these classes are apparently secondary, 94–98. — Development of secondary Semitic roots in general; general observation as to the use of inflective elements in the formation of secondary roots, 98, 99. — Predeterminative letters discussed in the order of the Hebrew alphabet, 99–102. — Indeterminatives, 102–106. — Postdeterminatives, 106–111. — General results of the inquiry: some of the predeterminatives originally vowels, others mere breathings, and the rest inflective formatives, 111–113. — Indeterminatives partly breathings and partly the result of inner vowel expansion, 113. — Postdeterminatives most frequent; any consonant might be so used; some of them were once vowels, 113. — Many roots show no determinative letter, having three consonants from the beginning; the composite origin of multi-literals is apparent, 113. —Forms with first radical the same as the last simply repeated the first radical, 114. — Roots consisting of but one consonant and a vowel, 114. — Semitic roots before the consonantal stage showed as great variety in formation as the Aryan, 114. — Scheme of possible and actual root-forms in Proto-Aryan and in Proto-Semitic, 114–116.

V. — COMPARISON OF ROOTS, ... 117–171

Difficulty at the outset in reconciling the different functions of the vowels in the roots of the two systems, 117. — Considerations leading towards a reconciliation, 117–120. — Roots adduced for comparison must be ideally represented by their consonants alone, 120. — Kinds of roots to be used; exclude alleged or suspected onomatopoetic or interjectional roots; take only those which express primitive notions, 120–121. — Value of the evidence according to these conditions, 122. — Use of etymological analogy, 122.

Comparisons made of words relating to *fire*, 122–125; words for *shining*, 125–128; words for *cutting* or *separating*, 129–136; words for *rubbing* and *bruising*, 136–140; words for *uniting*, 140, 141; *stretching* or *extending*, 141–147; *bending* or *curving*, 147, 148; various kinds of *movement*, 149–152; *position*, 152–154; *shutting* or *enclosing*, 154, 155; *guarding against* or *fearing*, 155, 156; *binding together*, 156, 157; *pressing* or *crushing*, 157, 158; *carving* or *graving*, 158, 159; *piercing* or *infixing*, 159, 160; *wetting* or *pouring out*, 160; being *cold*, 161; *thinking*, 161, 162; *knowing*, 162–164; *being* or *existing*, 164. — *Noun-forms* of less evidential value, 164, 165. — Words for *horn*, 165; for *field*, 166; for *wine*, 167. Pronominal or demonstrative roots not to be profitably treated, 167, 168.

Tabular view of the comparable forms, 168, 169. — Closing remarks, 169–171.

RELATIONS

OF THE

ARYAN AND SEMITIC LANGUAGES.

CHAPTER I.

PAST AND PRESENT TREATMENT OF THE QUESTION.

THE subject-matter of the Science of Language has been rescued from the confusion and uncertainty which marked its superstitious and mythical treatment in pre-scientific times. The general methods and principles of its right comparative study are well ascertained and universally acknowledged. In accordance with these principles and methods certain families or classes of speech have been clearly established; and the work of classifying the various dialects of the world is steadily advancing with the progress of exact knowledge and critical investigation. There are two main tests whereby the relationship of languages, or families of languages, may be discovered or confirmed: the comparison of structural features, and the comparison of roots. The former criterion finds its application in the attempt to show that the languages in question have in common their leading types or modes of expression as these are revealed in their flectional and syntactical characteristics; its principles are those of Comparative Grammar, in the strict sense of the term. The latter criterion is employed in the endeavor to prove that the idioms compared possessed in their primitive state the same working vocabulary, by reducing their current vocables to their radical forms and primary meanings; its principles are therefore those of Comparative Etymology. Both of these methods are legitimate in their respective spheres, for they aim, with equal deference to established laws, to reach fundamental forms of expression as a basis of comparison. The grammatical test is naturally surer than the etymological; since forms of thought as expressed in the categories of grammar are more directly and palpably indicative of a common mental history among the speakers of language. This is so mainly for two reasons: First, grammatical features are found by experience to be more permanent and less easily transferred than verbal expressions; and this distinction we are bound to regard as valid for the pre-historic as well as the accessible forms of any groups of languages which may come up for comparison, so that it must hold equally good for the hypothetical proto-grammatical and proto-radical periods of them all. Second, the conditions of the rise and vicissitudes of grammatical features are better understood than the conditions of the production and early fortunes of roots. There is, to be sure, a great deal that is obscure in the former sphere; but in the latter nearly everything, as we shall see later, is a matter of dispute. For these reasons, and because such rapid and triumphant progress has been made in the province of comparative grammar as a test of linguistic relationship, it has lately become widely the fashion to uphold the exclusive validity of this criterion, and to declare that the resemblance, or even the identity (if it could be proved), of the stock of roots in different families of speech is of itself no proof of real affinity. Of course, it is admitted that where grammatical analogies prevail, etymological coincidences furnish valuable confirmatory evidence of ultimate identity, and so far they may be regarded as accrediting relationship. But investigators are seriously warned against regarding such evidence alone as being of any value whatever in this department of the science of language. The present essay is an attempt to remove some of the odium which attaches to the theory thus impugned.

Before going further, however, it will be necessary to lay down two principles upon which the validity of all the subsequent reasoning will largely depend. First it must be understood that all comparative linguistic reasoning furnishes only probable evidence, not demonstration of the kind that is said to be mathematically certain. The conviction of the earlier identity of forms compared may rise to the height of moral certainty, but this can only happen through the accumulation of probabilities. Even in the strongest kind of proof, namely that afforded by the analogies of grammatical forms, there is a "metaphysical possibility" that accepted conclusions may be erroneous : and the invincibility of the arguments in their favor is only due to the extreme unlikelihood that early speakers, from any chance or combination of chances, or through any occult operation of consentaneous intellectual causes, should have been led to employ similar types of expression for the same forms of thought, without any co-operation in the production of such linguistic phenomena. The facts to be considered in making up the case are, (1) the ultimate phonetic identity of the forms compared, (2) together with the degree of resemblance in the ideas expressed by these forms, and (3) the number of cases in which such resemblances are traceable in essential forms as compared with the extent of the whole field of investigation. Precisely the same classes of facts are to be adduced when the roots of two or more families of language come up for comparison. In both kinds of investigation we have to do with the weighing of probabilities. The evidence may differ in degree in favor of the former sphere of comparison, but it does not differ in kind. The methods of science are equally applicable to both departments, in the processes of selecting, sifting, analyzing, restoring, and re-adjusting. In both provinces the final comparison must be made only with the residuum of the last analysis, and then the decision rests upon the inherent probabilities in each case.

The second position to be upheld as a necessary preliminary is that in all the processes of the investigation we must have regard only to the well-established facts and conclusions of science, and not to any theories and hasty assumptions that proceed from the philosophizing that is rife upon such subjects. The success of the laborer will here depend mainly upon the caution and discrimination which he exercises in settling the limits and the conditions of comparison, and the patience and judgment which he employs in tracing each current form and idea to be compared to their fundamental expression. His business is simply to ascertain facts; if those facts are established, the conclusions to be drawn from them will meet with acceptance or rejection according to what may seem to each critic to be the antecedent probabilities of the case. Then only can current theories as to the necessary conditions of primitive speech be admitted into court, and the testimony thus received may pass for what it is worth. It might seem to be unnecessary to state so formally what ought to be accepted as one of the common-places of all science. But the statement comes to be a necessity, when it is found that some of the most influential writers on the science of language maintain that the field of comparison is absolutely limited to those families of speech in which grammatical affinity can be shown to exist. They assert that the inflectional and syntactical features of any system of languages necessarily prevailed from the very beginning, and that idioms outside of the limits just designated must have been separate from the very first, from the very peculiarities of their structural type. They maintain that all language starts with the sentence and not with the word, and that single terms are therefore not eligible for comparison. They say, moreover, that as single sounds are liable to constant change, phonetic agreement among current roots would be a sign rather of a primary difference than of identity. These and other objections to the admissibility of the comparison of roots alone as a test of relationship will be considered in the next chapter, and will be shown to be either half-truths of science or mere hasty assumptions of a premature linguistic philosophy. What it concerns us now to maintain is that the field is the whole world of speech, and that judgment is to be passed not upon attempts to go beyond restrictions arbitrarily laid down, but upon results arrived at after a strict application of the methods of science to the materials chosen for comparison.

The statement of the true method of procedure in this sphere is very simple. What the investigator has to do is to make the comparison of Aryan and Semitic roots after the forms chosen for the purpose have been reduced to their simplest expression. That is, they must be proved to be actual roots in their respective idioms, and they must be treated as expressing the root-idea. This, however, involves a careful study of the principles of root formation and development in the two systems in their primitive individual history. That is to say, we must deal not with current roots found in the Aryan and Semitic families of speech, but with Proto-Aryan and Proto-Semitic roots; and these must be eliminated according to the laws which are found to prevail in their respective spheres. In the following brief review of the efforts heretofore made to harmonize the Aryan and Semitic languages, the theories will be judged according to the canons just laid down. That most of the theorists have failed to secure even a patient hearing from many leading linguistic scientists is due in great part to the fact that they have almost wholly disregarded these axiomatic principles.

The whole period covered by attempts to settle the general problem before us might be properly divided at the point of time when comparative philology was established as a science. Previously to that epoch the question cannot be said in strictness to have had a history; for there is no history where there is no law of progress. But even in the later era we shall have to distinguish between those theories which have been advanced without regard to the just demands of science, and to those which show more or less deference to its methods as well as its spirit. Before the science of language was founded, even in its broadest outlines, it was impossible that any intelligent view of the subject could be reached. Even the very conditions of the investigation could not be apprehended. Theories the most vague and unsupported were held as to the relations of the various dialects of human speech. Previously to the close of the last century, the comparative treatment of languages was usually only a sort of philological alchemy, in which Hebrew roots played the part of the philosopher's stone. Instead of regarding the several idioms of the world as developed from decayed and germinal forms, one language, accessible only in the literary and cultivated periods of its history, was venerated as the common source of all the rest, and languages the most diverse in structure and in typical character were believed to have been developed naturally and gradually from one of the least flexible and versatile of all forms of speech. This notion was based upon the persuasion that the oldest records of the race must have been composed in the earliest language, and that the most sacred of all tongues in its history and varied associations must have been the form of speech bestowed upon man at his creation by the gift of his Creator. Originating among the teachers of the synagogue, we know not how early, it was embraced by the Fathers of the Christian church,[1] and held almost undisputed sway until the comparison of languages became a subject of sober inquiry.[2] During the Middle Ages, when the rabbins engrossed the study of the sacred languages, and continued to illustrate the congenial theory of the antiquity and originality of the Hebrew tongue, there was not the interest or the knowledge in the Christian church that would have been necessary for its intelligent criticism. In the period between the revival of learning and the development of the science of comparative philology, there was, indeed, occasional objection to this venerable doctrine; but it was based rather

[1] Gregory of Nyssa, however, surmised that the Hebrew was one of the languages that arose out of the confusion at Babel. Orat. contra Eunom., xii. Quoted by Franz Delitzsch, Jesurun, p. 48.

[2] Theodoret, Philo Judaeus, and some of the rabbins regarded the Aramaic as the more ancient idiom. This, however, is only a sort of collateral theory. Theodoret supposed that the Hebrew was a special divine revelation to Moses.

upon its general improbability, than upon definite scientific evidence. During this period, also, a modification of the old opinion grew into some favor; according to which the Hebrew was held to be, if not the source of all other languages, at least the most ancient, and the one which preserved with the least degree of change the original stock of roots, and therefore the standard with which the verbal forms of all other tongues should be directly compared. The doctrine, in the one or the other of its general forms, was held very tenaciously; and, etymology being rather an art than a science, or rather an art founded upon no science, the task of comparison and assimilation was a very simple affair. For, as the expounders of the theory could not be refuted by an appeal to established laws of relationship between the various forms of speech, they were free to cite at pleasure mere coincidences and fanciful analogies as proofs of true affinity, and thus to vindicate the supposed sacred prerogatives of the Hebrew tongue; being opposed only by the smiles of an incredulous few, which they could afford to ignore, as having the support of nearly all who were interested in the subject. This dogma, so long and widely and firmly held, has now no more than a historical significance, and needs no labored or formal disproof. It is sufficient to remark that the Hebrew has no claim to consideration, in this connection, above its Semitic sisters or reputed Indo-European cousins, and that its long ascendency has been due, under the conditions of erroneous linguistic principles, simply to its high antiquity and the circumstance that it is the best known and the most highly venerated of its ancient family, by reason of its sacred associations. The Highlander and the Welshman, who affirm that their respective dialects have also a claim to be considered the primitive languages, have much of the same kind of evidence to adduce as that which has always been advanced in behalf of the Hebrew; and they, in their turn, might be met by a strong array of striking analogies, presented with equal confidence, as proof that the idiom of the Sandwich Islanders should not be left out of sight in any candid examination of the question.

It will perhaps be proper to illustrate the methods of this system of comparison by a few instances selected from the works of writers in recent times, and even in the present century. They will forcibly suggest the great advance made in linguistic science within the last sixty or seventy years, and may also serve as a warning to any who may still insist on a radical affinity between verbal forms on the evidence of mere external resemblance.

We find the acute and learned Moses Mendelssohn [1] among the later serious advocates of the doctrine that the Hebrew is the parent of all other idioms. Matthias Norberg,[2] a respected scholar of the early part of this century, after close scrutiny, detected in the Greek language the inherited lineaments of the same venerable and prolific parent. According to him, ἔθνος arose from עם, a people, by the insertion of θ; λόγ(ος) was transposed from קול, a voice; μυθέω, was changed from מָשַׁל, to liken. But the most frank and hearty exposition of the theory that we have seen is a little book by the Rev. Alexander Pirie,[3] a man of considerable linguistic attainments, but of still greater ingenuity. We cite some of his numerous derivations. He supposes that our word *bog* comes from בכה, to weep or run with water; that *boggle* (bogle) is connected with בהל, as inspiring terror; and that *tar* is derived from תאר, to mark, as being much used for marking sheep, sacks, etc. From רגם he would deduce the Latin *rego*, because stoning was an exercise of the supreme authority as a judicial punishment. In his opinion, גמל, "to retribute," gave rise among the Hebrews to the word *camel*, on account of the revengeful disposition of that animal.[4]

[1] In prolegomena to his edition of the Pentateuch, cited by Delitzsch, Jesurun, p. 46.

[2] See Friedrich Delitzsch, Indogermanisch-Semitische Wurzelverwandtschaft, p. 3.

[3] A Dissertation on the Hebrew Roots, intended to point out their extensive influence on all known languages (Edinburgh, 1807). The introduction, written by another hand, says of the author, "had he never lifted his pen on any other subject, the following pages would establish his character as a scholar and a Christian."

[4] This derivation, however, it should be remarked, was once quite common.

RELATIONS OF THE ARYAN AND SEMITIC LANGUAGES. 9

גנב, to steal, gives the origin of our word *knave*, which "at present is used in a bad sense, the same in which the Hebrews used it." Comparing Solomon's description of his spouse as "a garden inclosed," he imagines that גנן includes the idea of beauty, which is guarded with peculiar care, and that hence arises the Greek γυνή; while "the cognate Latin *genita*, a daughter, is plainly the source of our *Janet*." דין or דון, to judge, gave birth to a numerous progeny. δέον, what is just, and δεινός, skilled (in judging), do not surprise us very much; but we are further asked to accept δίνη, whirlpool, or whirlwind, "from the idea of vehemence in pleading." And, as the judgment-seats of antiquity were often groves, δένδρον is added to the family, which is next increased by the accession of our English *den*, because oracular judgments were frequently delivered from caverns. For a similar reason any hollow vessel came to be called a *tun*, "the *d* being changed into *t*, as usual." As a judge held a distinguished station, the Spanish *Don* is next admitted to the domestic circle; and since דין also means to dispute, and "as people in angry dispute are still said to be teethy, or to show their teeth," it was thought inhospitable to leave the Latin *dens* chattering outside in the cold. גלה, with other meanings, has the sense of carrying away captive. "Now the א prefixed forms a noun; before נ it sounds *ang*, hence the Teutonic *angel*, with its cognates." The confusion of tongues at Babel arose, he says, from a defect of labial utterance. When one would have said *Bel* (בעל), he said *Babel*. Hence also our word *babble*. He is very sparing of onomatopoetic affinities; but he would probably concede to that class of analogies the relation he holds to exist between the Hebrew עני, sorrow, and *och hone!*

These instances, though perhaps more whimsical, are not more unreasonable, than many of the combinations that have long been held, and are still to be met with in current literature. We find a writer so recent and influential as the late Albert Barnes stating, in his popular commentary on Job, that our word *evil* comes from the Hebrew אֱוִיל. It is surely necessary, in view of such facts, that the general principles of the science of language should be made an essential part of a liberal education, at least to such an extent that one will not need to be a specialist to be able to detect and disprove such inaccuracies as these.

But we must now consider the more safe and sober attempts that have been made to compare the two great families before us. The study of the Sanskrit, which afforded a clew to the mazes of the varied forms of Indo-European speech, was also the occasion of a more just appreciation of the conditions of the problem we are considering. In that ancient language, so perfect and intelligible in structure, large numbers of Aryan words were detected in their most elementary accessible form, revealing to the acute and delicate perception of such men as W. von Humboldt, Grimm, and Bopp the laws which determined their modification into other varieties of expression. Science having thus vindicated her claim to this vast province of speech, it was felt that other districts — nay, the whole realm of human language — must also be subject to her of right. Henceforth the reign of fancy and caprice in these affairs was at an end; and their intrusions would always be unwelcome to the new *régime*, though they could not always be repelled. In the treatment of the relations between the two great families of speech, now clearly established and defined, as well as between the several languages in each, it was felt that laws regulating all changes of form must be sought and assumed to exist, and hence also that the utmost caution must be used in the comparison. This, we mean to say, was the tendency of the method of inquiry, and the professed aim of the several investigators. Some, however, while recognizing the necessity of this principle, have failed, unconsciously, to act upon it, being frequently led to violent and capricious assumptions through their eagerness to attain the final theory of solution. Others, again, influenced either by dogmatic prejudices or by a conservative temper, have refused to indulge in any speculations upon the subject, or go so far as to assert that the languages themselves, as well as the races they typically represent, can never be proved to have been originally identical.

With regard to the earliest portions of the present period, we have chiefly to remark a tendency to bring Semitic words into close connection with the widely-related and hospitable Sanskrit. Adelung's Mithridates, the monumental boundary-mark between the old and the new regions of philological research, holds also a certain dividing-place in the history of the present question. Its learned author was the first to compare, to any extent, the Sanskrit with the Semitic vocabulary. As to his method, however, he is to be placed wholly within the old unscientific period. Not being himself a Sanskrit scholar, he was the more inclined to the prevalent error of comparing full-grown words, and not roots, or even stems, in the languages discussed. He connects, for example, the Sanskrit *ádima*, first, with the Hebrew אָדָם, Adam.

Some of the greatest pioneers of philological science, also, with all their sagacity and penetration, were carried beyond the limits of probability in their theories, or rather conjectures, upon this subject. Being not, in general, Semitic scholars, and their survey being necessarily rapid and superficial, their analysis was not sufficiently profound to deter them from assuming close relations to exist between forms which had only a casual and external resemblance. The tendency to assimilate the two idioms, excited by the magnificent results of the comparison of the several Aryan languages, may be inferred from the fact that even W. von Humboldt accepted a multitude of the most superficial combinations as proving an essential affinity between the forms compared. Bopp, also, attempted to establish a number of analogies which must be called forced and arbitrary; though that great philologist was unwilling to guarantee the absolute correctness of all his conclusions on this subject.

As we are now approaching the latest period of the investigation, and shall have to speak of the comparative value of theories largely influential at the present time, we may refer in passing to an opinion advocated at one time by Lepsius and Benfey and more positively asserted by Bunsen (in his Outlines of the Philosophy of Universal History, and elsewhere). The view held by them was, in general terms, that the Semitic and Aryan families are related to one another, and have as intermediary the Coptic, or rather the ancient Egyptian, as representing the North African group of languages. The leading arguments were, that the striking resemblances and analogies between the grammatical forms of the Coptic and the Semitic pointed clearly to a connection between those languages, while the fact that many coincidences were found between Indo-European and North African vocables created a presumption in favor of an early relationship between these also. In the defence of these positions Lepsius[1] and Benfey[2] wrote special treatises, and the same theory was maintained by the Egyptologist Schwartze in his work on Ancient Egypt (Vol. I. 1843). It is doubtful if the survivors of this group of theorists would now maintain this doctrine, at least as far as the Indo-European family is concerned.[3] And it must be allowed that the verbal resemblances between the Indo-European and North African families of speech are too sporadic, and apparently too superficial, to warrant any serious attempt to compare them in the present state of science. The question of affinity between the Semitic and North African families is still undecided.[4]

Gesenius, the great lexicographer, and inaugurator of scientific Semitic studies in Germany, maintained, in general, a neutral attitude towards the problem before us. True to the empirical principles of his philosophy of language he refrained from dogmatic generalizing while he could not make

[1] Zwei sprachvergleichende Abhandlungen (1836.)
[2] Das verhältniss d. ägypt. Sprache zum semitischen Sprachstamm (1844).
[3] With regard to Lepsius it may be inferred from his last work, Nubische Grammatik (Berlin, 1880), p. iii ff., that his present views on the question of the classification of languages exclude the above theory.
[4] The theory is discussed unfavorably, from his philosophical point of view, by Renan, Histoire générale des langues sémitiques (4th ed., Paris, 1863), p. 80 ff., 456 f. Cf. the more intelligent and liberal remarks of Sayce, Introduction to the Science of Language (London, 1880), p. 178 ff.

certain progress towards fixed underlying principles of unity. It is true that both in his Manual-Lexicon and in his Thesaurus he has instituted a vast number of verbal comparisons with Indo-European forms, which have helped more than all else written upon the subject to bring the question before the minds of ordinary students, and to affect their opinions regarding it. But he refrained from presenting dogmatically a theory of these analogies, being inclined to believe, until further light should be thrown upon the problem, that they were the result either of an early contact of the races leading to an exchange of vocables, or of onomatopoeia, or of mere accident. It should be remembered, however, that his sentiments on this subject were formed before modern science had reached those of its grandest conclusions which might well justify still broader assumptions. Yet he adopted and amply illustrated a theory whose establishment would tend towards the solution of the problem — the doctrine, namely, that the triliteral Semitic stems were reducible to significant and fundamental biliteral roots contained in the first two consonants; the last letter exerting the special modifying influence that determines the meaning of the word. In large numbers of these ultimate roots he discovered close correspondences with Indo-European forms, which, however, he declined to accept as conclusive proof of internal relationship.

We come now to consider the opinions of two authors whose opinions have been so fully elaborated as to entitle them to be considered the founders of a special school[1] of Semitic philology. We mean Julius Fuerst[2] and Franz

[1] The "Analytico-historical," so-called, because, on the one hand, according to its principles, the various elements of language and of individual words are held to be endowed with inherent significance which is to be determined by a profound analysis, and because, on the other hand, they call to the aid of their investigations a body of Jewish tradition, such as the Targums, the Talmud, the Masora, and the later Rabbinical writings. The name serves to distinguish their system from the so-called "empirical" school of Gesenius, and the "critical" or philosophical school of Ewald. These terms have now little significance, as they serve to designate tendencies or principles rather than well-defined sects or parties.

[2] Lehrgebäude der aramäischen Idiome mit Bezug auf die indo-germanischen

Delitzsch,[1] theorists whose vast learning and patient industry it is impossible not to admire, but whose philological system it is equally impossible to accept. In it the process of verbal analysis for the purposes of comparison with analogous forms is carried to its greatest extreme. The chief monuments of this system are the Jesurun of Delitzsch and the Woerterbuch of Fuerst; the former an exposition and defence of its principles; the latter, the repository of its practical results. Their leading positions may be summarized as follows: (1) That all languages have been developed from one common stock of elements, all of which, in every part of speech and in every word, have a significance, definite and divinely imparted. (2) That this innate idea is to be educed through a minute analysis of each form, and the widest comparison with the forms of other dialects of the language of mankind. (3) That the Sanskrit is the master-key to unlock the secrets of all Aryo-Semitic speech, there having been originally one "Sanskrito-Semitic" idiom, from which proceeded six families of speech — the Sanskrit, the Medo-Persian, Semitic, Graeco-Latin, Germanic, and Slavonic. They thus annul the ordinary classification, and make all the Semitic dialects together a sister idiom to each member of the great Aryan division. (4) That, accordingly, the chief resort for purposes of comparison is the Sanskrit, while the other related languages should also be consulted as supplementary and illustrative. (5) That all Semitic triliteral forms can be traced to original biliterals, parallel to the most numerous class of Sanskrit roots, and being the significant element in each form, as containing the original and typical idea. (6) That the remaining portion, the determinative modifying element, consists of a suffix, or, far more frequently, a prefix, corresponding in meaning, and as nearly as possible in form, to the Sanskrit prepositions. In the elucidation of this system they have subjected a vast number of forms to examination

Sprachen. Leipzig, 1835. Librorum Sacrorum Concordantiae. Leipzig, 1840 Hebräisches und chaldäisches Woerterbuch. Leipzig, 1857–61.

[1] Jesurun; sive Isagoge in grammaticam et lexicographiam linguae Hebraicae, contra G. Gesenium et H. Ewaldum. Grimmae, 1838.

and have besides illustrated their conclusions by citations chiefly from authors of the rabbinical school, the products of whose fancy they have elevated to the dignity of scientific demonstration. The objections to the whole theory are obvious: (1) The reduction of the triliteral Semitic roots to biliterals is too through-going and mechanical. Analysis does not always yield biliteral roots; nor is it to be expected that it should. Triliterals, as well as biliterals, have existed from the beginning. (2) The combinations attempted with the so-called sister tongues are not made upon any sound etymological principle, nor are the forms reducible, in many instances, to anything like even external resemblance. The following comparisons may be cited as evidence (Jesurun. p. 175), טָהַר, to be pure, with Sanskrit *çrâ* and Lat. *cremare*, to burn; טָמַן, to conceal, with Gr. μένειν, and Lat. *manere*, to remain; כָּבַשׁ, to subdue, with Skr. *pad*, to go, and Gr. πάτειν. (3) The prepositional additions which are supposed to have been prefixed to the biliteral roots do not preserve any fixed and certain meaning in the various instances cited as illustrations.

The views of Ewald, the greatest grammatical and historical genius among the Semitists of the last generation, are deserving of consideration. As might be expected, they are original and unique. Employing his special faculty of investigating the nature and relations of grammatical forms, he endeavored to prove by researches in the Indo-European, Semitic, North African, and (so-called) Turanian families of speech, that these are outgrowths of a common stock, which is most nearly represented now by the Indo-European. A discussion of this view will have to be made in the second chapter, when we come to consider the question of criteria of affinity particularly. It is sufficient to say in the meantime that the evidence adduced in its favor is precarious in its very nature, and therefore inconclusive. He made subordinate the question of the relations of special words or predicative roots, though he maintained the possibility of such combinations, and a considerable number of comparisons may be gathered from his various linguistic writings, all of them ingenious, but none of them convincing, because not based upon a systematic theory. Singularly enough, for a man of his insight, he failed to trace such words to their primary expression.

An ambitious and laborious effort was made by Ernst Meier, in his Hebräisches Wurzelwörterbuch (1845), to construct a dictionary of Hebrew etymology, upon a theory which must be pronounced extravagant and on all grounds untenable. His main position was, that the stock of roots in the two families might be reduced by analysis to a mere handful; that the Semitic forms, which are currently larger than those of the Aryan division, might be brought to a primary conformity with the latter, by throwing off from each of the triliterals a letter which was regarded as secondary. Such letters were supposed to have been developed in accordance with an assumed principle of reduplication in the formation of verb-stems, analogous to that which prevails in Aryan perfects. That is to say, one of the primary letters might be repeated in the formation of the stems of the Semitic perfect tense, and this was followed by the adoption of the developed forms as current roots. Since, however, the repetition of the same sound was felt to be disagreeable, the secondary letter was dissimilated from its primary in most cases, though the limit of choice was confined, in each instance, to its own class of sounds.[1]

The most laborious and persevering investigator of the subject in recent times is Rudolf von Raumer, who is also well known through his Indo-European researches. The reader will find his theories succinctly stated in his latest contribution.[2] He has considered it a necessity to establish laws of phonetic representation regulating the changes undergone by roots that appear in both families. These are as follows: (1) The hard Semitic explosives or mutes are represented etymologically by the corresponding Aryan sounds; (2) the soft Semitic explosives are mostly represented by the

---

[1] Cf. Friedrich Delitzsch, op. cit. p. 8.
[2] Zeitschrift für sprachvergleichende Sprachforschung, xxii. p. 235-249. Compare also D. Pezzi: Glottologia aria recentissima (Turin, 1877), p. 37-41.

hard Aryan sounds of the same organs. On these assumptions it is obvious to remark that there is no regularity in the alleged correspondences. It follows from his principles that the Aryan *t*, for example, may be represented either by Semitic *t* or *d*; *k* by *k* or *g*; *p* by *p* or *b*. We do not maintain, in the meantime, that this cannot be a fact; but it is evidently not in harmony with the observed facts of other languages that are mutually related, in which the mutes as well as other sounds are either equivalents, or are differentiated according to laws normally invariable. As Von Raumer's scheme is without observed analogy, very strong evidence should be adduced in its support before it is entitled to acceptance. But in the combination which he makes for the purpose of proving his assumed laws he does not advance much beyond his predecessors. He seems not to have kept in mind the consideration that, if the two families were ever one, they must have separated before the full-grown noun and verb stems in each system were developed; for he commits the error of failing to search for Proto-Aryan and Proto-Semitic roots, as furnishing the only basis on which lawful comparisons can be made. His combinations are in general only a little less improbable than those of Fürst and Delitzsch, referred to above. His assumed phonetic laws are, therefore, still unproved.

The Italian scholar, G. I. Ascoli, has given the weight of his great name to the general theory of an ultimate relationship of the two families. He has, in letters addressed to Bopp and A. Kuhn and in contributions to scientific journals in Italy, also attempted to bring forward special evidence for this doctrine based upon the resemblance between certain formative elements (case-endings, etc.) in the respective systems. In this he follows close upon the track of Ewald, though in a narrower field, and the nature of the proof is equally uncertain with that adduced by the latter. He also deals with the well-known similarities between some of the numerals and most of the pronominal stems, a subject to which Lepsius had before him given special attention.

The inherent difficulties of this branch of the investigation are that we do not know the roots of the numerals, and that the further back we go to their primary forms the less resemblance they seem to show; while as to the pronouns, as we shall see later, the phonological investigation is somewhat uncertain. The testimony from this source is, moreover, too general to be universally satisfactory, since several pronouns are alike in a great many other families of speech. Ascoli has also formulated laws of phonetic change. To Von Raumer's rules he adds a third, to the effect that an Aryan *g* is represented in Semitic by פ. The evidence given for this is scanty and precarious.

The most scientific and also the most satisfactory attempt to prove an Aryo-Semitic relationship is undoubtedly that of Friedrich Delitzsch, in his Indogermanisch-Semitische Wurzelverwandtschaft (1873). As to his general attitude towards the question, he is fully convinced of the hopelessness of attempting to reconcile the divergent grammatical systems; but holds it to be a possibility, that at some remote period, before any flectional tendency was exhibited in either, they possessed a common stock of roots. In seeking to ascertain the roots which may be shown to have once been the same, he recognizes the principle that we must aim to draw them only from the original languages from which the two families arose respectively. In making up the list of dialects from which the original Semitic language must be constructed, as far as its roots are concerned, he rejects the Old Egyptian rightly and the Assyrian wrongly. His view as to the latter appears (p. 29) to have been, that for lexical purposes Assyrian roots could not afford any essential help in the solution of the problem. But his own valuable labors since then in the interpretation of the cuneiform inscriptions have only confirmed the justice of the claim, long since put forth, for the independent character and essential importance of the Assyrio-Babylonian branch of the Semitic family.

When Dr. Delitzsch comes to the treatment of the roots that are eligible for comparison, he shows an advance upon his predecessors in the endeavor to employ a systematic theory as to the constitution of those roots. Taking advantage of the labors of Indo-European investigators, such as Curtius and Fick, he assumes as valid the distinction made by them between primary and secondary roots, according to which the latter differ from the former through the possession of one or more determinative letters, which represent, according to a sort of phonological symbolism, modifications of the radical notion (p. 33 ff.). His views on this branch of the subject seem to be philosophical and sound. In taking up the Semitic roots, he shows evidence of not having made a careful and thorough analysis. He proposes to throw off the old limitations occasioned by the theory of biliteral as distinguished from triliteral roots, according to which the former are eligible for comparison with outside languages, while the latter are not. But that he is really controlled by that theory is plain from his classification of Semitic roots (p. 43 ff.). He draws the line broadly between roots with "weak" and those with "strong" letters. In the former class the weak letters are claimed to have little or no essential significance, while in the latter each letter is primary and autonomous and the forms containing it may be put directly on a level with the Aryan roots. Now what are these insignificant weak letters? We find that along with א, ה, and ו, the same unimportant part is assigned to ח and ע. Why ח should be excluded does not appear. It is no more and no less an original independent sound than ה or ע. But the radical error here is the assumption that because roots containing these letters are "weak" in the inflections, the sounds themselves must be adventitious and unmeaning. The fact is, however, as we shall show in our fourth chapter, that the weak letters are as independent and significant in their original forms as the strong, and that the determinative letters are no more taken from the latter than from the former. Again, the letter נ alone of the strong consonants is put in the same class with the weak letters when it appears as the first sound in roots. But the true view of the matter is that the weak letters may be used as true predeterminatives along with the strong letters נ, שׁ, and ת, since each of these is found to occur at the beginning of secondary roots as the modifying element.

The views of Dr. Delitzsch as to phonological representation should also be subjected to some criticism. In seeking to prepare a scheme of correspondences in sounds (pp. 82, 83), he commits the error of neglecting to reduce the phonetic stock of both systems to the limits that obtained in the original languages. With regard to Aryan sounds, indeed, he confines himself to those which have been accepted by phonologists without dispute, as belonging to the primitive idiom; but in the Semitic family he takes the sounds just as they stand, only grouping together, for the purpose of bringing out a set of equivalents to the Aryan sounds, those which are organically the most closely allied, without investigating the question of their true historical relations. For example, he assumes that the Hebrew צ, where it answers to the Arabic ض, and the Ethiopic ፀ, is to be classed with ד, all of them representing the Aryan *d* and *dh*; while the Hebrew צ, answering to the Arabic ص, and the Ethiopic ጸ, is to be grouped with ס, שׂ, and שׁ, as representing in common the Aryan *s*. The fact is, however, that the Arabic ض, and its Ethiopic analogue appear to have been developed far more frequently from a radical צ than from a radical ד. The question of the production of these letters is surrounded with great obscurity, but this much is plain.[1] Further, his system divides sharply between the different kinds of Semitic gutturals. Thus, the Hebrew ח, with its Semitic representatives, historically corresponding, as he claims, with the Aryan *gh*, leads one division of sounds: while א and ע with their representatives form another, answering to the Aryan spiritus lenis. Here ה is thrown out altogether, although it is a

---

[1] Thus, ፀ as the first letter of Ethiopic roots (see Dillmann, Lexicon Aethiop. col. 1322 ff.), appears to come in only one case certainly from an original ד, while it is sometimes actually developed from a primary שׁ.

sound at least as fundamental as ח. To be consistent he would have had to represent it also by the Aryan *gh*, which would have been self-evidently erroneous. The true view is that all the Semitic gutturals (except א, which is common to all languages), are of pure native origin, and are capable of an organic classification which precludes the possibility of the theory we have criticised.

That these errors should detract in many cases from the value of the comparisons of roots made by Dr. Delitzsch was inevitable. Moreover, there is a want of consistency observable in the application of these laws. Thus, in comparing the Heb. שְׂרִיף, a thin board, and its Arabic hometyma, with Gr. σκάπ-τω, to shave off, he remarks (p. 76), that "there is nothing surprising in the agreement of the aspirated *ḥ* with the Indogermanic *k*," though, as we have seen, he sets forth the same ח sound as being the representative of the Aryan *gh*. In the choice of roots for comparison it is unfortunate that so many of them, perhaps the majority, are liable to be objected to on the ground that they may be of onomatopoetic origin, and therefore more likely to have arisen independently in the separate history of each family. In spite of these and minor defects, the work is of much value from its stimulating and suggestive character, as well as from the actual contributions it makes to linguistic learning.

Another German scholar, J. Grill,[1] has taken up, with much acuteness and ingenuity, the question of the relations of the two families from the stand-point of the constitution of their roots. Recognizing the divergence not merely of flectional characteristics, but also of root-structure in the two systems, and emphasizing the fact that in the Aryan root the vowel is coördinate with the consonant, and that in the Semitic it is subordinate, he seeks to harmonize the two by carrying the view back to a hypothetical period when a so-called "Alpha-sprache" prevailed, whose peculiarity was

---

[1] Zeitschrift der deutschen morgendländischen Gesellschaft, Vol. xxvii. pp. 425–460. Ueber das Verhältniss der indogermanischen und der semitischen Sprachwurzeln ; ein Beitrag zur Physiologie der Sprache.

that *a* was the only vowel sound employed in either. This view will be taken up, and shown to be improbable, when the same problem is to be dealt with in the course of our own investigation.

In addition to the names of special investigators already cited, general mention should be made of some of the greatest lights of linguistic science, who with more or less confidence favor the doctrine of the possibility of a real relationship between the two families, though they have not attempted to formulate any special scheme for harmonizing their divergences. On this side may be put the names of Eugene Burnouf, Max Müller, Pictet, and Steinthal. The opinion of the last-named is specially valuable, because he has discussed [1] the question on general linguistic principles more thoroughly than any other of those who have not entered into an analysis of vocabularies. On the other hand, the probability, and even the possibility, of such affinity is rejected upon general principles by an influential, and perhaps at present the dominant, school of linguistic philosophers, who either hold to the theory that languages of different inflectional types are necessarily of diverse origin, or on general anthropological evidence favor the doctrine of the diversity of human species. Among the most pronounced of the opponents of any scheme of reconciliation are Pott, Schleicher, Renan, Friedrich Müller, and Sayce. Their views will necessarily be considered in the next chapter, when we come to take up more particularly the question of the criteria of relationship.

[1] Zeitschrift d. deutschen morgenländ. Gesellschaft, xi. 396 ff.

CHAPTER II.

CRITERIA OF RELATIONSHIP.

IN passing now from the more critical to the more constructive portion of our Essay, it will be well to throw some light on the nature of the task before us, by exhibiting the more obvious points of contrast between the two families of speech.[1] Bringing thus into view the distinguishing features of each idiom, we shall be the more able to propound the conditions of a just investigation, and to establish the true criteria of evidence as to their relations.

In every language, or group of languages, there are three elements, whose peculiarities determine its special character, and help in different degrees towards its classification. These are, its sounds, its structural principles, and the contents of its vocabulary. In the case before us the numerous points of dissimilarity seem at first sight radical and indicative of a diverse origin, while the points of agreement appear accidental and superficial.

As regards the first element, the sounds of the respective languages, great divergence is apparent among the dentals, in which the Semitic family has developed a strong tendency to multiply sibilant and lisping sounds, and a wider differ-

---

[1] Comp. Ewald, Ausführliches Lehrbuch der hebräischen Sprache (8th ed.), 1870, p. 26 ff.; Renan, Histoire générale des langues Sémitiques (4th ed.), 1863, p. 18 ff., 454 ff.; Whitney, Language and the Study of Language, p. 300 ff.

ence still among the gutturals, in which the same family exhibits an astonishing variety of phonetic expression.

On examining the roots and the general structure of the words, we are at once struck by the strange and unique principles that control the Semitic dialects. While in the Aryan family, roots may consist of a consonant and a vowel, or of two or more consonants accompanying or grouped about a vowel, it is an almost invariable Semitic law, that the roots of nouns and verbs, so far as the analysis of living forms can testify, are based upon three consonantal sounds. As to Semitic words in actual speech, we see exemplified as universally the peculiar principle that the vowels are used to express subordinate, modified, or accessory notions, while the consonants, which form the framework of the word, embody its fundamental idea. Again, this family has only to a small extent the habit or capacity of compounding words, a circumstance which tended to multiply the number of its roots, while the Aryan languages, having developed that principle largely, were enabled to economize their original stock. Further, the more strictly grammatical features of the two idioms appear to be no less radically divergent. Renan characterizes the Semitic grammar as a sort of architectural and geometrical structure, as contrasted with the latitude and flexibility that mark the inflections and syntax of Aryan speech. In the Semitic verb there is a great variety of forms ("species," *quasi* conjugations) to express modifications of its general notion, which represent chiefly simple subjective conditions, e.g. causative, declarative, desiderative forms; while in its tenses, which are few, the more metaphysical idea of time is vague and indeterminate, and in those dialects which in a more reflective stage in the history of the race, attained to greater precision in expression, could only be definitely indicated by the help of limiting words. In the same way its moods are also few and entirely foreign in typical structure to those of the Aryan languages. With regard to its noun, the prevailing absence of case-inflections, and the formal modification before a limiting noun, called the construct state, are among the more obvious peculiarities. The objective personal suffixes of verbs, and the possessive personal suffixes of nouns are further important characteristics of the Semitic family.

Within the sphere of the lexicon, also, we are not led, immediately at least, to unmistakable marks of real affinity. If the stock of roots in the respective vocabularies was originally the same, the evidence of this does not appear on the surface.

The leading differences between the two families being thus indicated, the character of the problem to be solved becomes more intelligible. The following mode of procedure will perhaps be the most natural and serviceable. After a glance at the question of phonetic phenomena, the grammatical features of the respective systems will be taken up and it will be considered particularly whether there is a possibility of reconciling the divergences outlined above. After estimating the results of this inquiry it will be necessary to decide whether any other criteria have a right to be admitted, and an attempt will be made to show that the comparison of roots alone is not opposed to the true methods and principles of linguistic science. These discussions will form the subject of the present chapter. It will then be proper to take up the two systems separately, without reference to the question of harmonizing individual words, the object in view being the obtaining of primary forms that may be legitimately compared. This will involve, first, a reduction of the sounds of each family to their original limits and expression, and, second, the presentation of a scheme of phonetic representation. The treatment of this subject will comprise another chapter. Then it will be necessary to treat of the constitution of the roots of the respective systems according to the laws that prevail in each. The concluding portion of the work will then be taken up with the comparison of roots, chosen and dealt with according to the principles that are found to underlie their production and development.

Taking up now the subject of the criteria of relationship,

a few words will have to be said on the subject of the sounds of the two families. As they stand, they do not accord, in so far as sounds are found in either system which do not appear in the other. The question arises: Are we to regard these differences as precluding any attempt to compare the stock of roots in the two idioms? Certainly not. The variants may not be original. Sounds are often found in languages in their modern or literary form which did not exist in their early condition; and sounds frequently appear in one or more of the branches of a linguistic family which the parent tongue did not possess. In the Aryan family, for example, there is not one of its branches which does not contain sounds foreign to the primitive speech, from which all in common sprang. It follows, therefore, that phonology is not a primary criterion of linguistic relationship at all. If, after reducing the phonetic stock of each system separately to its primary range of sounds, there are found in one system some which do not appear in the other, this fact is still not decisive of original diversity of idiom. An examination of the structure or of the verbal forms of each language may prove beyond a doubt a primitive unity, in spite of the phonological differences. Thus if we take the sounds of the Keltic group, as they are found to have existed in the original Keltic language, the gutturals which belong there are not represented in the Indo-Eranic idiom; nevertheless these two branches of the Aryan family undoubtedly came from one common stock. So the cerebrals in Sanskrit have not prevented the harmonizing of that language with the dialects of Greece. It appears, then, to be a false and arbitrary restriction which those scholars make who would prohibit any attempts to harmonize the Aryan and Semitic idioms, on the ground that the phonology of the two shows such distinct features.[1] It is not well to lay much stress on such differences; for that would be to appeal to an unsound source of

---

[1] E.g. Prof. A. H. Sayce, who tells us in his Principles of Comparative Philology (1874), p. 101 f.; Introduction to the Science of Language (1880), ii. p. 176, that the phonology of the two systems opposes the idea of their relationship.

comparison. Nor is it hard to account for the notorious fact of important changes in the phonology of any people. The influence of climate, food, habits of life, and external conditions in general upon the organs of speech, is both extensive and familiar; and it is easy to perceive why, through the course of ages, and long separation under different skies, each of the branches of one original language has often developed sounds quite unknown to the phonology of the other. The comparer may reduce the stock of sounds in each system to its limits as they appear to have been fixed in the original languages. If the sounds are then found to have been at one time the same in each, this settles nothing decisively as to the original relations of the systems compared. If, on the other hand, sounds are found to have existed from the earliest accessible period in either idiom which are not found in the other, this also proves nothing as to primitive relationship. It is the business of the comparer, in either case, to seek for laws of phonetic representation by the comparison of roots, not directly of sounds, according to which certain sounds in the one system may eventually be found to correspond with certain sounds in the other system. These sounds thus harmonized may be either approximate equivalents, or they may be such as analogy shows to be capable of representing one another through permutation in human speech. The main point to be insisted on here is, that sounds are not at all a primary criterion of linguistic relationship. It is sometimes forgotten or unperceived by glottologists that sounds are compared with one another only as they become the outward form in which ideas are clothed. Significant terms are the proper material of comparison, and the sounds are traced out, classified, and compared secondarily according to the history of the embodied thoughts. The direct and independent comparison of sounds is, properly speaking, a department of physiology. Those who put forward the theory just criticised might not maintain in general that a striking divergence in the phonology of any two systems necessarily precludes their original identity. This would be to contradict history. But when the two idioms in question are thought, on other grounds, to be radically separate, the phonological objection is as natural as it is fallacious.

We must now turn to the structural peculiarities of the two systems of speech. Here we shall have to regard the languages just as they appear in actual use, and inquire whether anything can be inferred as to their early condition. In other words, we must, by analyzing and comparing the verbal and syntactical forms, endeavor to reduce them to common primordial principles. In our previous Article we had hinted at the general value of grammatical comparison in this field of inquiry; but here it will be necessary to consider the question more at large.

The conditions for this investigation are both favorable and unfavorable. On the one hand we find the two groups based upon fully-developed inflectional systems. There is also abundant material, in the form of a large literature in both idioms, bequeathed to us by a long line of intellectual ancestors. Moreover, the internal laws of each of these types of human expression are sufficiently intelligible; for the principles of Aryan speech have furnished the more familiar elements of Comparative Philology, and the Semitic dialects, in their simple and regular structure, reveal easily the process through which their vocables are built up. But, on the other hand, we have this disadvantage, that we do not possess in either idiom literary remains that throw any direct light upon its primitive form. Go back as far as we may, we meet with only full-grown words, in whose complex sounds we seem to hear no more than a faint echo of the simple language of the world's childhood.

Taking up now the word and the sentence as the two main elements of human speech, and regarding the structure of both as the surest distinguishing features of a language or linguistic group, the inquiry naturally divides itself into two branches. First, as to the word, we may assume its special character to be exhibited in its typical form, as this is associated with the process of its development from the root. In this way, e.g. we may contrast the structure of *dictum* from *dic* with that of נִקְטָל from קְטַל, or *dicens, dicentes* with קוֹטֵל, קוֹטְלִים; noting such matters as the part played by the vowels in each set of words, as related to the function of the consonants, and the significance of the prefix or affix as entering into the inflectional system of each type of language. Secondly, we have to compare features of syntax; the Semitic sentence is placed side by side with the Aryan, and the endeavor should be to determine whether the existing forms can be reduced to a common system of expression.

Now, it must be acknowledged that hitherto such inquiries as these, conducted, as they have been in some cases, most acutely and profoundly, have had but ill success so far as their main object is concerned. The result, at best, has merely added to other presumptions in favor of an organic relationship, through the exhibition of a few analogies in the more fundamental structural principles of the word and sentence, which have, however, arrayed against them numerous divergences, apparently no less radical and essential. Our more definite conclusions, however, must be reserved until we have analyzed the evidence.

If we consider the structure of Semitic and Aryan vocables, we find the following to be, perhaps, the most striking difference : in the latter class the radical portion of the word is almost always modified by additions at the end, whether in the base forms of nouns and verbs, or in the various inflections to which these are subject; while in the former the principle of augmentation at the beginning is also followed, as, for example, in the formation of the species (conjugations) of verbs, of the future (imperfect or aorist) tense, and of a large portion of the derivative nouns. This fact is seized upon by Ewald,[1] who compares it with the

[1] Abhandlung über den Zusammenhang des Nordischen (Türkischen), Mittelländischen, und Koptischen Sprachstammes (aus dem Zehnten Bande der Abhandl. der königl. Gesellschaft der Wissenschaften zu Göttingen). Göttingen, 1862. The full title of Professor Pott's treatise, in which it was severely criticized, is as follows : **Anti-Kaulen ; oder mythische Vorstellungen vom**

predominance which the Coptic gives to prefixes in the formation of words, and infers from this, among other evidences, that the Semitic holds an intermediate position between that language and the Indo-European. He ascribes to this strong inclination for prefixes in the Semitic dialects the absence of terminal inflections in the nouns, or of cases, properly so called.[1] Yet from the circumstance that such elementary inflections as those that express person, gender, and number are formed through affixes, he assumes this to have been the original principle of formation. On this he rests one of his pleas for the acknowledgment of an original affinity with the Indo-European stock.[2] Not a very strong case, surely. Yet when we consider the intermediary relations which the Semitic seems to bear to the Aryan and the Coptic, the presumption upon this ground does not seem worthy of being slighted altogether.

We need, however, to look a little more closely into the structure of such forms in the respective types of language. When we examine an Aryan word, and arrive at what is considered the root, we find that the latter is transferred to a a derivative or to an inflected form without internal modification. In all cases, certainly, the principle is clear that the parts of the root are inseparable, and that its vowel as well as consonantal elements must enter into the combination. But the Semitic principle is totally different. The consonants

Ursprunge der Völker u. Sprachen. Nebst Beurtheilung der zwei sprachwissenschaftlichen Abhandlungen Heinrich von Ewald's, Lemgo u. Detmold, 1863. Although Professor Pott made an effective presentation of the more obvious difficulties of Ewald's system of comparison, neither his arguments nor ours have any tendency to lessen the merit of the permanently valuable portion of the treatise, in which, startling from fundamental principles common to both families (which appear to us probable, though to him as scientifically established), he has traced with unsurpassed penetration and ingenuity the structural development of the two idioms.

[1] The accusative and genitive in Arabic, and the accusative in Ethiopic bear no true analogy to the cases of like appellation in the Aryan tongues. On the indefiniteness of the like endings in Assyrian, see Schrader, Assyrisch-Babylonische Keilinschriften, p. 230 ff.

[2] Comp. § 107 c. in his Ausf. hebr. Sprachlehre.

which form the root or stem, while remaining themselves unchanged in their new relation, are separable, and may admit between them any of the whole stock of vowel sounds. Each of them, in fact, seems to be the centre of functional activity for itself within a certain range. Now, this divergence from the Aryan system seems to be even more radical than would be the assumed primitive correspondence in formative methods which we have just considered. It seems to be nearer the sources of the individual life in each system of speech, and therefore to be a more important element in determining their early relations. Thus we find that while from one plausible analogy we would be led to hope that a bond of union had been discovered, we are warned by a more searching analysis that the breach is wider than we had thought.[1]

From this one point of view, therefore, we seem compelled to abandon the expectation of proving a structural relationship, and unless stronger evidence is forthcoming from other

[1] Ewald does not seem to have recognized this necessary priority of more essential to more formal characteristics in these languages. He thinks that the formative elements in the Semitic family, where prefix and affix were both employed, largely determined the principles of "inner mutation in the roots" (Zweite sprachw. Abhandlung, p. 64). He says that these appendages, pressing equally before and behind, tended at last to force their way into the body of the root, thus favoring the internal play of the vowels as modifying elements. To this, he adds, the original divisibility of the root lent its influence. We would suggest that the relations between the formal appendages and the internal structure of the word are as follows: — The greater freedom in the location of these appendages in the Semitic words is a secondary influence, due to the independent existence assigned to each radical of the triliteral root, so that not the whole body, but the individual members decide the place of the external additions. Hence, while in the Aryan languages the influence of analogy would of itself be sufficient to cause these appendages to appear uniformly at the place first chosen, namely at the end, the same tendency could not be equally felt in the Semitic vocables; for each letter would assert its autonomy, and claim its rightful share of the tributary elements. Naturally the force of the middle radical was kept in abeyance by the two others, one on each border. But that this was due merely to the exigencies of its position, and not to its own quiescence, may be inferred from the fact that in the most highly developed of the Semitic tongues — Arabic and Ethiopic — this letter assumed a powerful modifying activity, and actually instituted a new and complex system of internal inflection — the so-called broken plurals.

sources, we must only fall back upon the hope of establishing an ante-inflectional affinity.

We have now to inquire whether there is anything in the syntactical features of the two forms of speech to justify us in holding to a radical affinity between them. This task seems even less promising than the one just attempted. The general aspect of the Semitic mode of expression seems to have nothing whatever in common with the typical character of an Aryan sentence. They are as divergent as the mental characteristics of the two families of which they are the expression. The thought in any given case seems to be cast in entirely different moulds.[1] In the Semitic period we are struck with the absence of qualifying and subordinate clauses; its parts are simply co-ordinated. There is nothing complex in its structure; all is simple and direct, both in the construction of the members of the sentence and in the arrangement of its words. The specific distinctions of importance are, the relative positions assigned in each to the subject and the predicate, the modes in which the sentences are united, and the ways in which they express the relation of dependent words. Now, the same difficulty meets us in this comparison as that which we encountered in considering the structure of verbal forms: as far back as we are able to trace the two idioms we find that they have preserved essentially the same modes of expression. Thus it is characteristic of the Semitic syntax, throughout its history, that in the ordinary, direct, simple sentence the verb precedes and the subject follows; while in the Aryan languages the reverse order is as prevailingly the rule. It may be surmised that the actual order in the Semitic idiom was not the original one, and that there, as in the Aryan sentence, the subject, as being the leading word, was in earliest times placed first. But this is incapable of proof. Ewald institutes a subtle parallel[2] between supposed changes in the

---

[1] The cardinal distinctions are delicately discriminated by Renan, Histoire générale, etc., p. 19 ff.

[2] Zweite sprachw. Abhandlung, p. 57; comp. p. 28 f.

verbal and in the syntactical structure of the Semitic language. He believes, as we have seen, that the formative elements in Semitic words were originally placed at the end, and that the principle of prefixing them was of later origin. He then affirms that in conformity with this process there was an early but gradual change in the order of the parts in the sentence, so that what seems to us to be the natural arrangement was inverted.[1]

The same ill-success seems inevitable in examining another leading distinction. The mode in which a dependent is joined to a governing noun in the Semitic, and which is found in all its dialects, bears no analogy to anything known in pure Aryan grammar.[2] That the first of the nouns should be modified, instead of the limiting one, is a principle essentially Semitic. Whatever may have been the origin of this construction; whether or not the vowel termination of the construct state, which is universal in Ethiopic, and has survived besides in archaic forms in Hebrew,[3] was the original bond of union between the words so related, the impossibility still remains of bridging over the linguistic interval between this and the Aryan usage, according to which, the second or limiting noun must undergo inflection, or be governed by a preposition.

With regard to the third leading distinction in the sphere of the syntax, we think that the simple co-ordinated structure of the Semitic sentence with the prevailing use of merely copulative particles, is not so radical or so inherent in the system as to furnish even the external conditions of linguistic comparison. It is due, as it appears to us, almost entirely

[1] That the Indo-European order is the most natural may be inferred from such primitive types of language as the Chinese. See Max Müller, Science of Language, i. p. 118.

[2] The employment of a similar construction in modern Persian, and in Armenian, being a usage borrowed from the Semitic, is no exception to this rule, any more than is the tendency to separate the letters of a word by the insertion of a vowel, which is shown sometimes in the first-named language, and has the same source.

[3] For opinions as to the origin of this termination, see Green, Heb. Gram § 198 a; Ewald, Ausf. hebr. Spl. § 211 a.

to the intellectual character of the people at the formative periods of their language. The Semites, as a race, have not been given to habits of reflection or to logical reasoning, delighting rather in the contemplation of the external features of the objects of sense and the more lively emotions of the soul. Hence the absence of inferences, of close definitions, and of special qualifications. The discursive faculty was but little employed, and required no special instrument for its expression.[1] But the comparison of the two idioms in this sphere would soon lead us from the study of the language to the study of the races themselves, and take us beyond our province.

Having thus attempted to outline a system of structural comparison between the two families of speech, it remains for us to sum up the meagre, yet instructive, results of our inquiry.

1. The two families are conspicuous among the languages of the world, through the possession of fully developed inflectional systems, as distinguished from the idioms called agglutinative, isolating, polysynthetic, and partly inflectional.

[1] The early inversion of the natural order of the elements of the simple sentence may have contributed its influence to the formation of Semitic style, as Ewald maintains (Zweite sprachw. Abh., p. 59), but probably only to a slight degree. Pott seems to be in error when, in criticizing Ewald, he says (Anti-Kaulen, p. 281), that the brevity and uniformity of the Semitic sentence are due to the paucity of adaptable conjunctions, and of moods and tenses, which would subserve a like end. For, if we look merely at Ethiopic, a Semitic dialect which *does* possess a marvellous capacity for the expression of logical and connected thought, we see that it possesses those grammatical elements to the requisite amount. The inference is then near at hand, that, at the time of its growth into a distinct language, these parts of speech were evolved from its quickened resources, in order to serve the purposes of an exceptionally active intellectual life among the people; there being also no doubt that much mental activity did once exist. See Dillmann, Aethiop. Gramm., p. 6 f.; Ewald, Ausf. hebr. Sprachlehre, p. 34 f. This conclusion, as confirmed to a certain extent by the history of the Arabic, would go to show that the Semitic type of expression was conditioned by the mental antecedents of the race, and not by an inherent inadequacy of the language. Of course, when the cruder dialects became old and fixed, they lost the capacity of development, and when employed for unaccustomed purposes, had to borrow the necessary expressions from foreign idioms, as is proved from the history of Aramaic and Talmudic Hebrew.

2. Without considering the question whether what are ordinarily called roots in the Semitic dialects are really ultimate significant elements, it is plain that the bases of verbal forms in the two families are essentially distinct in their structural principles. This dissimilarity is marked not simply in the phenomenon that in the Semitic idiom they are generally composed of three consonants, but more fundamentally, in the independent activity assigned to each of these letters.

3. With regard to the formative elements of living words, we saw that there was some reason to believe that in the most essential, and presumably the most primitive, of inflected forms, they were attached at the end of the roots, as in the Aryan languages. This, however, does not furnish, by itself, a very strong argument in favor of a grammatical affinity.

4. The syntactical peculiarities of the two systems, as would naturally be expected, do not yield more favorable results, following, as they do, upon structural principles themselves divergent.

We are thus left without any direct demonstration of relationship from this source of evidence. The question then recurs: What, if any, is the residuum of testimony, from a structural comparison, in favor of the theory of the original unity of the two systems? It is to be feared that no answer, universally satisfactory, can be given. In some minds the common possession of an inflectional system would of itself create a strong presumption of an identity of origin. And when to this fact is added what has been alluded to with regard to the intermediate position of the North African family of languages, whose inflections hardly rise to the dignity of a system, but betray, when they do exist, a marked resemblance to the Semitic, the inference seems proper that the families last named went hand in hand in the earliest stages of their history, and after their separation followed in very different degrees the structural impulses which all three idioms had received in a common home. But apart from this, and on general linguistic considerations, it does not seem likely that two such highly and fully developed systems of speech would have originated without a strong, even though very early, bond of relationship. They represent a supremely great achievement of the human mind, something unique in the history of men; and one is led to attribute a common impulse to the beginnings of each, as in the contemplation of the worship of the synagogue and of the cathedral we are led back to the one supreme religious idea that the world has known. The theory of an original diversity in the two families appears, in fact, to raise a more formidable difficulty than those which the doctrine of their unity occasions, because the psychological phenomenon which it would imply is less credible than the assumption of a divergence from a common idiom, which, before the separation, contained the germs of a grammatical system.

Yet this kind of evidence is both too general and too subjective to command universal assent. At best it affords a presumption, and not a demonstration. Although, therefore, we think that the two families of speech were still united when the first manifestations of the inflective impulse were felt, yet, as we have very little scientific proof to present, based upon grammatical comparison, it is only left to us to see whether there is not another kind of evidence available in the inquiry.

We are thus led to compare the verbal forms possessed by the two families, and thence to determine whether analogies between separate words are obtainable in sufficient number to justify us in regarding them as something more than mere coincidences. But at the outset we are confronted by arguments urged against the admissibility of such evidence by those who hold that the two idioms are radically distinct. It will be necessary to test the validity of such objections before proceeding further.

We are first met with the general plea that, as grammatical features are the proper marks of linguistic relationship, it is unscientific as well as futile to go behind them, and to compare the lexical contents of the two groups.[1] This declaration is sweeping and imperious. Against any plausible coincidences already brought forward it is always urged that they must be the result of chance or of onomatopoeia, or of some subtle intellectual analogy in the formative processes of early speech. Against those who make any systematic attempt to compare the two idioms on the basis of their respective vocabularies it is maintained that they begin at the wrong end. The failure of Bopp in his attempt to compare the Indo-European with the Caucasian and Malayo-Polynesian families of speech is paraded [2] as a proof of the exclusive sufficiency of the method of grammatical comparison, of which he had been the originator and expounder. Now, before considering the special difficulties raised by these theorists in the way of adventurous and irreverent investigators, we should say that these vehement protests against an alleged unscientific method are themselves not at all in the spirit of true science, inasmuch as, if universally heeded, they would stand in the way of all progress in the further comparison of languages. A stop would at once be put to all efforts to co-ordinate into special families those languages of the so-called Turanian group, which agree only in the agglutinative or combinatory character, just as the Aryan and Semitic families agree in being inflectional. And so for the the classification of other types of human speech. It may also be assumed that if the same spirit had been dominant at the beginning of the present century, those bold but happy

[1] So Renan, Friedrich Müller, Sayce, and other opponents of the theory of an original affinity.

[2] See Friedrich Müller, Grundriss der Sprachwissenschaft, I. Band (Vienna, 1876), p. 58. Comp. Benfey, Geschichte der Sprachwissenschaft u. der orientalischen Philologie in Deutschland. München, 1869, p. 511 ff. It is very likely that Bopp was inaccurate in many of his combinations with the above-mentioned languages; but on this general question of the admissibility of verbal comparisons, we cannot but respect very highly the judgment of the immortal founder of Comparative Philology. Here, as in his Glossarium Sanscritum (within the Aryan family), he was too hasty and liberal in the admission of analogies. But this was due to his method in practice, and not necessarily to the unsoundness of his theory, into whose conditions he probably saw as clearly and deeply as any dogmatic obstructionist of the present hour.

generalizations without which, perhaps, comparative grammar itself might not have been created, would have been denounced as unscientific. The great discoveries within the sphere of the Indo-European family have made it fashionable to believe that glottology has unfolded all its fundamental principles, while it is forgotten that only small districts of human speech have been explored and annexed to the domain of science. The reaction against the old lawless methods of comparison which now prevails is no doubt wholesome and just; but it is a question whether this one of its present forms ought, or is likely, to be permanent.

But, more particularly, it is alleged that we are bound to forego any attempt to assimilate the two groups, because (it is said) science has established the fact that the various types of speech now known rest upon a primitive diversity of origin — that language was developed at first from numberless dialects, and not from a common source. Now if this dictum were conceded to be indisputably true, it would not settle the question at issue; for we should next have to determine what constitutes the primitive type in any given case; in other words, whether the two inflectional families of the world's speech may not have arisen from one original dialect. Such an issue is not necessarily excluded by the conditions of the supposed fact of linguistic history. For the limits of each early type or dialect must be settled in one or both of two ways: by appealing either to the evidence of the science of language, or to that of comparative ethnology. If we refer to the former, we find this at least, that these two families are the only ones that have a fully developed inflectional system; a fact suggestive of a possible primitive bond between them. If we appeal to the latter, the evidence is decidedly unfavorable to those who maintain a diversity of origin. The Semite differs but little physically from the Aryan, and resembles the European more than the latter does a Hindoo. This is acknowledged by Renan, one of the most influential of the class of writers alluded to, who admits that the current distinction is based chiefly upon language, and affirms that, viewed from the physical side, the Semite and the Indo-European form but one race.[1] The consideration that the two systems of speech together now occupy so much of the earth's surface does not come into conflict with the assumptions of the theory we are considering; as though the doctrine necessarily involved a certain ratio between the primitive extent of a language and the number of its present speakers. It is only maintained that the original dialects of mankind were numerous and diverse, it being an essential part of the theory that but comparatively few of the early stock now survive, the rest having been eliminated in the struggle for existence, It should also be remembered that, so far as we can judge, the primitive Aryans and Semites must have comprised only a relatively small portion of the earth's inhabitants, and that it was their inherent intellectual and moral superiority that secured their gradual progress, and their survival of the vast civilizations that preceded them.

Hence we see that no real advantage would be lost if the theory of the original multiplicity of language could be proved. Still, as it might seem to justify a presumption that each present great division of human speech had a separate beginning, it may be proper to say a few words upon the subject of its pretensions.

Those who maintain this polygenetic theory of language are usually disbelievers in the doctrine of the common origin of mankind. But we do not need to assume that they are prejudiced to any extent, by their views upon the latter question. formed upon other grounds than the results of linguistic research. Some eminent linguistic scholars think that the final decision of the question as to the original unity or diversity of language rests with physical science.[2] Others maintain that ethnology and the science of language should not be mixed up together.[3] However this may be, we have

---

[1] De l'origine der langage (4th ed.). Paris, 1864, pp. 204, 208.
[2] E.g. Benfey, Geschichte d. Sprachwissenschaft in Deutschland, p. 789 f.
[3] E.g. Max Müller, Science of Language, i. p. 326 f.

now to consider simply the worth of the linguistic proof which the advocates of the theory of a primitive diversity of dialects have to offer.[1]

The argument upon which reliance is chiefly placed may be stated as follows : — Although it is natural to the human mind to seek for and to expect unity of origin in all forms of existing things, the facts of linguistic history point us to an opposite conclusion with regard to the development of language. It is a fact that widely-spread idioms owe their predominance to the influence of civilization; that if we turn to savage tribes (among whom are certainly to be sought traces of the earliest modes of Nature's workings), we find an endless diversity of dialects, each village, sometimes, having an idiom of its own; that if we go back to the earliest records of written speech, we see the same conditions exemplified, as in ancient compared with modern Greece; and that a number of subordinate considerations (which we cannot here adduce) strengthen and illustrate the position thus assumed. Since, therefore, as far back as we can go in the history of language we meet the same diversity as at present, or even a greater, it is only in accordance with the methods of science to conclude that it was always so.[2]

But surely it is only scientific to draw like inferences from like conditions. It is surely a perilous assumption to regard the conditions of the formative periods of language as analogous to those of its historical progress in the latest ages of the earth. Apart from the peculiar physical and psychological factors that *must* have entered into the formation of early speech for a long period, there is one possible

[1] The theory is maintained elaborately by Sayce, Principles of Comp. Philology, chap. iii., "Idolum of primeval centres of Language"; Renan, Orig. du Lang. chap. viii.; Hist. générale des langues Sémitiques, p. 93 ff.; cf. Pott, Ungleichheit menschlicher Rassen vom sprachwiss. Standpunkte, p. 201f. Fr. Müller, Grundriss der Sprachwissenschaft, p. 50 ff. A neat statement of the general position is given by Schleicher, Compendium d. vergleich. Grammtik d. indogermanischen Sprachen, 1866, p. 2 f.

[2] On the origin and growth of dialectical differences in contravention of the above general theory, see Whitney, Language and the Study of Language, p. 177 ff., and in American Journal of Philology, 1880, p. 341.

difference of vital importance which is assumed not to have existed. It is regarded as an unquestionable fact that language *could* only have arisen when mankind had become very numerous and scattered. Passages might be cited from some of these writers [1] which imply a contradiction of this position; though it is clearly the corner-stone of their whole theory. The assumption must be either that man sprang from a vast number of beginnings, so that mankind originally constituted different varieties; or that language is not an essential faculty of man, but was produced at a late period. When these doctrines are *proved*, we may be compelled to accept the theory, but not until then.

Let us see, however, what is the evidence really afforded by the conditions of savage life. If we take a general survey of any large country, peopled within historical times by savage tribes, we are at once impressed by the great multiplicity of dialects. But if we regard these tribes at successive periods of their history, we do not find that their dialects diminish through the course of time, but that with the spread of population they themselves increase. Hence, if we cast our glance backward beyond historical times, we can see that there must once have been in that country only, at most, a few primordial idioms. This surely follows, unless we assume that the communities of such a country were originally more numerous than at present. Now let us look at the matter from another stand-point. We see that in large districts, or even in a whole continent (as in North America),[2] only one general type of language has prevailed among the aborigines. But the historical diversity of dialectical expression is most easily explainable from the consideration that under such conditions of life there is always an impulse to unbounded variety, and especially that such an impulse must have been strongest with the first uncertain beginnings of speech. The inference therefore seems unvoidable, that within such a *habitat*, at least, the

[1] As when Renan (Orig. du lang. p. 182), says that each group of men formed its language upon a foundation laid "par une tradition antérieure."

[2] But a few of the Central American dialects are said to be of the isolating type.

42 RELATIONS OF THE ARYAN AND SEMITIC LANGUAGES.

Babel of present dialects is reducible to one original type. We are not now attempting to show that *all* the varieties of human speech may be brought under one form; we only claim that the same conditions which could bring about the development of the American (polysynthetic) dialects from one primitive idiom might also have educed all the Aryan and Semitic fully inflected dialects from one primordial centre. This possibility, certainly, is in no danger of disproof from a theory which would determine the conditions of the childhood of language by the regulated growth and ample scope of its vigorous youth, and can discern in the mysterious and far-distant past nothing but a copy of the familiar phenomena of the present.[1]

We have now to consider the difficulties suggested by the advocates of another theory, capable as we think of a more scientific defence. We are brought into contact with it in this way. When it is admitted that the grammatical features of the two forms of speech cannot be assimilated, and we proceed to consider the possibility of a comparison on the ground of verbal analogies, we have to assume that before the development of an inflectional system there was a more rudimentary form of speech, in which only the mere roots were employed, or, more definitely, in which there was no exemplification of the categories of root, stem, and base. The nearest approach to such a linguistic type is the Chinese language, whose vocables are capable of being used for any

[1] Many of the subordinate arguments employed by these scholars involve the same fallacy. Thus Renan (Orig. du langage, p. 177 ff.), lays great stress upon the fact that the terms employed by early tribes to designate their neighbors were usually derived from some notion implying the unintelligibleness of their language, they being usually styled "stammerers," "dummies," or some other such unsocial designations. He cites in confirmation such words as the German *Walh* (Welsh), the Sanskrit *Mleccha* (supposed to be cognate with the former), the Greek *Aglossoi* and *Barbaroi*, the Abyssinian *Timtim*. He then proceeds to argue that language must have been *originally* divided no less impassably. On this it is obvious to remark that we do not know whether these terms in all languages did not arise after the diverging dialects had become mutually unintelligible from familiar causes. Further, many of the cases are taken from within the Aryan family; and it is now certain that there was once a time when all those who used that idiom could make themselves mutually understood. To this opinion Renan himself elsewhere (op. cit. p. 49 ff.), professes his adherence.

of the parts of speech, and which attains a perfectly adequate capacity of expression, merely through the relative position of the words, and the use of a small number of particles. But there are some who would forbid us to assume such a hypothetical Aryo-Semitic type of language, and who maintain strenuously that it is both improbable and unexampled; that it has no ground in linguistic philosophy, and no analogy in the history of speech. It is maintained by them that no language has ever passed from an isolating stage (as above described) into an agglutinative or combinatory, and none from either of these into an inflectional. Probably the strongest assertion of this dogma has been made by E. Renan and A. H. Sayce, in their works already cited. The question is so vitally important to our discussion, that it demands a serious, though necessarily a brief, consideration. We shall therefore present the best evidence we can in favor of the theory of the development of each of the families from a more primitive type, considering the opinions and objections of opposing theorists as they may occur to us in connection with different points in our argument.

Our theory as to the divarication of the two families rests upon the doctrine that every inflectional language must have passed through a simpler combinatory stage (of longer or shorter duration), which itself arose from an original isolating type. In our grammatical comparison of the two systems we did not think it necessary to discriminate between the first two stages, both because in these languages the combinatory period appears to have been comparatively brief, and because the structural divergences seemed so radical as to exclude the probability of a common form of speech after the process of combination had once begun.[1] The evidence for this may be gathered from what has been said of the modes in which the formative elements of fullgrown words are attached in each group, as well as of the differences in their internal structure. We have to go right back to the most simple and primitive type of language,

[1] Comp. Max Müller, Rede Lecture on the Stratification of Language, Chips from a German Workshop (Eng. ed.), iv. p. 102.

and we think the step may be justified demonstrably by proof that each system has been developed from a more rudimentary condition. As to the psychological causes which led to the adoption of the more complex forms of expression, we admit that they are to a large extent mysterious, but claim that they are not without historical exemplification. As to the occasions which led to the perpetuation of each system, after its origin, we hold that they are easily discoverable, and are being constantly repeated in the history of human speech.

We would remark, first, that we have an exhibition of tendencies in many languages which clearly reveal the possibility of such development. It is said, however, that there is no instance of a clear transition from one state to another. Certainly there is not; nor have we any right to expect that, after the forms of a language have been hardened through the course of ages, they could be changed easily and speedily. We do not claim, however, that any language has made this decisive transition under conditions similar to those with which we are now familiar. But it is manifest that in the early state of every form of speech, the possibilities of such a serious change were immeasurably greater. In those times men were seeking after suitable forms of expression, not having at hand any that had been gradually worked up into a familiar and adequate instrument of thought. One class of them would attempt, by various devices, to perfect, without radical change, the primitive rudimentary type, a task in which they succeeded admirably, as we learn from the adaptability of the Chinese to an unlimited range of ideas. Others would adopt the expedient of combining their roots; and this idea was carried out apparently in two main directions. Among the founders of the so-called agglutinative languages, predicative roots were modified (so far as we can determine) generally by other nominal and verbal forms; while the pioneers of inflectional speech made as decided a choice of demonstrative or pronominal roots to accomplish a similar end. In the former case, since both elements of the new compound stood out with equal prominence, they would naturally retain their former importance, and oppose persistently the inevitable tendency to phonetic corruption; while in the latter the comparative unimportance of the determinative elements would subject them to the predominance of the radical portion, their individuality would, after a time, become lost in the consciousness of the speakers, and phonetic decay having one begun, the process would soon extend itself to the whole body of the word.

So much for the general process by which these complex systems were educed from the primitive condition of simplicity. The force which operated in each system to produce uniformity of structural type throughout its whole extent must have been chiefly the powerful influence of analogy. How potent this was in early times we may infer from its power even within historical periods, as we learn from the development of varied forms in such idioms as the Romanic languages, and most conspicuously, perhaps, in the dialects of France. And we maintain that the possibility of a transition from the isolating to a combinatory stage in early ages, ought not to be more difficult of conception than the change which has actually taken place in the development of the modern analytic out of the ancient synthetic languages. We must remember that men were groping after more complete and satisfactory modes of expression. They had not yet lost the spontaneity of primeval speech, and with an inherent, almost creative, facility they could achieve without reflection that which, to us, would seem to involve a radical intellectual change. When the superior fitness of the new principle of formation was once perceived, the whole family in which the change began would assimilate its speech with equal readiness to the forms of the more deserving system. The condition of things was very different after these aggressive principles became dominant. Each family, having moulded for itself a suitable instrument of thought, then *possessed* it. It did not seek any other, since it did not feel the need of it. Hence, we do not find in the accessible forms of language, the very earliest of which is much later than the period we are describing as essential to the development of each family of speech,[1] any instance of a complete transition from one type to another; nor should we expect it. The faculty of language is drawn upon only at need. It does not even furnish new words, unless these are required for the expression of new ideas; much less should we look for the creation of new grammatical categories without necessity. Yet we do find languages, some of whose features seem inexplicable on any other theory than the one we are advocating. We have such idioms as the Finnish, which are almost as much inflectional as agglutinative.[2] We have that most puzzling of languages, the ancient Egyptian, about which scholars hesitate to say whether it should be called isolating, agglutinative, or inflectional.[3] But of more importance than these facts are the peculiarities of some of the languages classed as isolating, such as those of Thibet and Siam, which partake largely of the combinatory character, while the Chinese itself, in some of its forms, exhibits a marked tendency in the same direction. If such mutability is manifested in languages checked in growth and fixed in general type through age, tradition, and usage, what must have been the capacity of radical change inherent in the earliest forms of speech, with all their simplicity and vagueness!

Our next argument is based upon the fact that an exami-

[1] It will be seen from what has been said that we consider all languages, from isolating to inflectional, to have undergone this, so to speak, subjective process of development. We must not make the mistake of assuming that all languages have started from just such a state as that now represented by the Chinese. This language itself must have passed through important changes in modes of expression before assuming its present condition. It is not a primeval language, but only a more primitive type of language than those familiar to us. A study of its system would show that it presents the result of a considerable psychological development.

[2] The approximation of agglutinative to inflectional idioms is of secondary though considerable importance. The psychological interval between these conditions is not nearly so great as that between the isolating and the combinatory stages.

[3] Comp. Whitney, p. 342 f.; Renan, Histoire générale, p. 83 ff.

nation of fully-formed words in Aryan and Semitic speech attests the doctrine that they are ultimately due to the accretion of originally independent forms. The determinative elements added to the roots have been ascertained in a vast number of cases, and shown to possess a significance of their own. The natural assumption is, that the same is true of all the original compounds. In the Semitic family, where the process of analysis is peculiarly easy, this conclusion may almost be taken for granted. But the advocates of the opposite theory prefer to consider the Aryan languages, where, confessedly, there is much more that is obscure in the ultimate constitution of some of the more primitive forms. Even with regard to these, however, the same presumption is probable. We are told,[1] indeed, that as far back as we can trace the Aryan languages they are inflectional, and, beyond that, they must be remitted to the province of physical science, which, as we are told with great confidence, could only prove that the brain of the earliest Aryan was capable of originating no other type of language. But surely this is claiming too much. Inductive reasoning has surely something to offer on the opposite side. While explanations of forms hitherto obscure are continually being made, we feel a strong presumption that if we could only penetrate the mist through which the opening dawn of Aryan speech is faintly discernible, all that remains mysterious would yet be brought to light. If these elements are always significant, it would be certain to the ordinary mind that they were once used independently — a conclusion which would establish our theory.

Such a conclusion, it may be said, is only an inference from a partial analysis, and not a demonstration based upon the working of a universal principle. Even if this were to be conceded, there is another way of considering the general question which leads to the same result. It may be shown that the opposite theory is psychologically inconceivable. The formative elements were originally significant, or they

[1] Sayce, Principles of Comparative Philology, p. 158.

were not. If they were significant, they were previously independent vocables. If they were not significant, how account for their employment as determinative symbols in the earliest attempts of the race to achieve an intelligible method of oral communication? Now, it is maintained (by Prof. Sayce) that although (as proved) later forms in these languages arose through the attachment of significant terms, or fragments of these, yet the *example* of inflection in the earliest periods was set in the creation of forms which conveyed in one single word both the fundamental and the modifying idea, the latter being expressed by "unmeaning terminations."[1] Thereafter, as the needs of the languages demanded, the progress would be easy to the attachment of significant terms. Which of these two theories has the greater inherent probability may appear from a candid presentation of the assumptions demanded by each. According to the one theory, at the very birth of these languages, when, as we are bound to assume, men were just accomplishing the task of giving forth in sound intelligible signs for the objects of nature and the simplest qualities and actions, we are to believe that they expressed the various *relations* of these by attaching to the phonetic expression of the root-idea (which must itself have been held on precarious probation) any one of a number of mere grammatical symbols, these having no existence save in such combination. It is natural to suppose that the earliest efforts of speech were, at best, not very easily understood, and that at least the relations between various objects would at first have to be indicated by various contrivances, such as gestures or other outward signs. But to attempt to express such relations by drawing, on occasion, upon a number of arbitrary (since not significant) sounds, would have tended very much to discourage incipient vocal communication. The other theory assumes

[1] Op. cit. p. 151. The words are evidently equivalent to "suffixes of little meaning" (p. 145, note). The use of the latter phrase may show how difficult it is to conceive of the growth of inflection by the attachment of unmeaning sounds to the root. In Prof. Sayce's Introduction to the Science of Language, 1880, I. p. 85, cf. p. 119, a similar theory of Ludwig (Agglutination oder Adap-

that at an early period, though not the earliest, of a given inflectional language, terms which had already grown familiar to the speakers, gradually came to have their various relations expressed by the combination with them of other words which were already accepted vocables; that at first those of early origin and of most frequent usage, such as demonstrative particles, were employed; that thereafter, as the circle of ideas widened, more special expressions came into use; and that in course of time, the sense of the independence of the two elements being lost, the word became one indivisible form in the popular consciousness. The choice lies between these two hypotheses, and only these; and hesitation between them does not, antecedently, seem possible.

But a very plausible argument is presented, to the effect that the farther back we go in the history of inflectional languages, the greater complexity of structure is to be found, while their tendency always has been, and still is, to greater simplicity, and we are therefore to assume that the primary types of expression were synthetic. Here again there is a fallacy, due to the failure to pass from the observed facts of accessible forms of language to the necessary conditions of its early development. The assertion that inflectional languages are continually becoming more analytic in their structure is based upon the phenomena of idioms that have received a literary cultivation, analysis being the necessary accompaniment of reflection, and the result of a self-conscious endeavor to attain greater simplicity and clearness of expression. Yet it may readily be conceded that back to a very remote period in the history of any such language the assumed conditions did exist. But the argument is valid only against any who might claim that throughout the progress of such an idiom a tendency to greater complexity prevailed. This, however, is not the position maintained here at all; for a multiplicity of complex forms is

---

tation, 1873), is cited and supported by the researches of M. Bergaigne into the nature of the Aryan case suffixes. In this instance he acknowledges more fully the difficulties attending both theories.

just what we would expect to have happened after the combinatory impulse began to manifest itself, in accordance with what we know of the general diversity and confusion of early efforts at language-making. Afterwards when any language became fixed in its structural type, and was much employed in the expression of manifold thought, the simplifying process was equally inevitable.

A more particular form of the same general objection to the root-theory has yet to be considered, and in it an extreme seems to have been reached in the way of crude philosophizing. We are told that language begins with sentences, not with words; that an idea cannot be communicated by the use of single words, and that even in the most primitive utterances of men such single terms had to be eked out by gestures or other signs so as to convey the ideas intended to be expressed; that the form in which such utterances were made characterized each linguistic type, and was perpetuated unchangeably in the development of the language; that the sentence is the unit of significant speech, and it is therefore evident that all individual words must once have been sentences; that the student of language therefore cannot deal with words apart from sentences.[1] Many considerations oppose this reasoning, any one of which is fatal to its sweeping conclusions. In the first place, even if it is admitted that spoken language can never consist of the use of a mere word without some form of predication concerning it, it does not follow that such a *form* is permanent from the first, and becomes crystallized about the word with its earliest utterance. On the contrary, since we know that the first means whereby men conveyed their ideas about objects, or the qualities of objects, must have been the employment of some kind of outward sign apart from the words that expressed those objects or qualities, these mechanical symbols of gesture, tone, and so forth, must necessarily have varied with the habits and genius of each community, while the names of the objects or qualities, once settled upon, would

---

[1] Sayce, Introduction to the Science of Language, Vol. i. p. 111-116.

become more permanently held in their essential phonetic representation. Such words, being conceptual, were perpetuated, their permanence being derived from the intellectual judgment that established them. The supplementary elements in the primitive utterance varied with each group of speakers or each community that helped to popularize and extend the much needed vocables; these demonstrative expressions being spontaneous, natural, and easily understood, were not permanent just because they were variable. It is unnecessary to point out how the reasoning employed is out of harmony with what is observed of all organization either in nature or in human history. The elements of the assumed "sentences" are all before us, each of them a separate entity; but the theory denies that there was any synthesis in their combination. It is as unphilosophical to assert that words could never have had an independent origin and history because in actual speech they are always found organized into sentences, as it would be to maintain that oxygen or nitrogen never had a separate existence because they are regularly found in definite combinations. The main fallacy, however, lies in the abuse of the term "sentence," as a grammatical category, in its application to the simple utterances of the makers of language. The stereotyped forms of fully developed speech could not possibly have been represented in such primitive expressions. If it is said that every utterance implies a sentence; we deny the statement, if the implication is that every utterance is capable of a formal grammatical analysis; for an intelligible expression can be made by the use of but a single word. When it is said that every such word would need to be accompanied by signs to indicate its bearing or special use, we reply that such signs as gesture, tone, and facial expression are not language at all, that is, not human speech; and with anything beyond this science has nothing to do.[1]

[1] Even taking these theorists on their own ground we can find much that proves the root-theory as against the sentence-theory. Thus we know that in a simple sentence the copula is of late origin in all languages, being usually an

These observations, which are all we have space for here, will show how little reason there is for accepting the *dicta* of Renan [1] that " languages issue ready made from the mould of the human mind," and that linguistic " families appear as established types once for all."

adaptation of the late metaphysical conception, to be or exist; and that in such widely separated idioms as Hebrew and Sanskrit, as well as in many others, in such expressions as "this is a tree," the copula was primarily not employed, the form being, "this a tree." Such an example shows how near even highly developed tongues still lay to the source of their individual life; and when we add to these considerations the fact of the ambiguity in the use of demonstrative pronouns in the early literary stages of such languages, the same example points us almost directly to a " sentence " and a word in one.

[1] Origine du langage, pp. 99, 116.

CHAPTER III.

COMPARATIVE PHONOLOGY.

IN dealing with Aryan and Semitic sounds as they come up for comparison, three questions present themselves in the following order. The first is: Does a marked difference in the current phonetic stock of the two families properly preclude all discussion of their ultimate identity? The second is: Will a fair examination of the sounds of the two idioms result in showing that the dissimilar elements have arisen in their respective systems from more primary sounds? The third, which is entirely distinct from the second, is: How do the Aryan and Semitic sounds represent one another in the accessible forms of hypothetical Aryo-Semitic speech? The first of these questions was answered in the last chapter, where it was shown that sounds are not a primary criterion of relationship. The answer to the other two questions will be given in the present chapter.

Our first task will accordingly be to take up the contents of the Aryan and Semitic alphabets, eliminate the sounds which may be proved to be secondary, and thus reduce them independently to their primary limits. Two practical results will thus be gained: we shall be able to determine what were the Proto-Aryan and Proto-Semitic sounds in which their earliest vocables were clothed; and we shall be able to reduce to its primary form any root that may come up for comparison containing sounds that are proved to be secondary. Of course the present discussion has nothing to do with bringing together the sounds of the two systems, and determining whether they corresponded to one another in actual Proto-Aryan and Proto-Semitic speech. That is a question to be settled apart. At present we have to take up the phonetic repertory of each family and reduce it to its primary limits irrespectively of other considerations. In this endeavor the chief work will have to be done in the Semitic department. Aryan phonology has progressed so rapidly and surely, in keeping with Aryan etymology, that although there is still dispute on some points of minor importance there will be no great difficulty in presenting a correct working scheme of ultimate Aryan sounds. It is hoped that the attempt will be equally successful with the Semitic alphabet.

The first class of sounds to claim our attention is the gutturals. The development of these in the Semitic languages especially is remarkable, particularly in Arabic and Ethiopic. That these were not all employed from the very earliest stages of Semitic speech, but were gradually produced in later times, can be made to appear at least very probable from the following considerations. In the first place we have the notorious fact that when we compare together roots which were undoubtedly Proto-Semitic, agreeing in other sounds but differing in their possessing different gutturals, an agreement or resemblance of meaning is shown in an immense number of cases. This seems to point to the conclusion that many of these forms were modifications of these synonymes through a variation of the guttural elements, a process which throws light on the production of such sounds in earliest Semitic times. Again we have the analogies presented by other languages. Thus within the Aryan family, which started with no true guttural, these sounds have been variously and sometimes strongly developed, notably in the Keltic and Armenian branches. So also in some of the American dialects.[1] In the next place, we must remember that in the growth of Semitic speech with its peculiar structure,

---

[1] Prof. Haldeman in Proceedings of the American Oriental Society, Oct. 1874 (Journal, Vol. x. p. ciii).

RELATIONS OF THE ARYAN AND SEMITIC LANGUAGES. 55

it was inevitable in attempting to express the great variety of notions bred in the minds of an intellectual people, that they should employ a greater variety of sounds than those with which they at first started. There was a two-fold inner necessity for this. First, the vowels could not be used in forming new roots among the Semites, but only in forming derivatives, or in expressing different aspects of the root-idea. Secondly, there was no compounding of words with prepositions or other modifying terms to express new relations or kindred notions. When the need for various expression was felt, resort must have been had unconsciously to the stock of consonants, from whose fundamentally distinct sounds there gradually arose variations, at first, perhaps, slightly, and finally quite strongly marked. Other causes no doubt conspired with these in each case of differentiation, and we think it probable that the strongest gutturals, such as are met with both within and without the Semitic family, were produced by those general influences, such as food, climate, and mode of life, which led to their development in the Armenian and both of the great Keltic dialects. But we think that these finer distinctions, peculiar to the Semitic, such as the Arabic ح and ع, as well as some of the non-guttural variants, were due not only to such occasions, but to those others which are peculiar to Semitic speech. Hence, as it appears to us, the immense range of consonantal expression shown in the Semitic idiom, exceeding anything in the pure Aryan languages, even the Sanskrit,[1] some of whose sounds (the "cerebrals") are possibly borrowed, and others mere euphonic variants. But, in the third place, however we may account for the variety of consonants, the fact of the gradual development of the different sounds does not rest entirely upon theory. We can trace the process of development in the later stages of development. The Arabic ع is not found as a fixed independent sound in the other

[1] Max Müller's Science of Language (Am. ed.), p. 180, gives the number of current Sanskrit consonants as thirty-seven.

dialects, not even in Ethiopic, which went hand in hand with it so long after the other dialects left the parent stock. We can see a tendency to its use in Hebrew, or rather a pronunciation of the ע somewhat resembling it, since we find the ע sometimes represented by the Greek γ in proper names in the Septuagint, even in the middle of a word when it is usually not represented at all (e.g. ῥέγμα for רעמה, Gen. x. 7). But this only shows how it was possible for the Arabs to develop an occasional into a fixed sound,[1] and so throws light upon the subject of the origin of the Semitic gutturals generally. In Hebrew one character stood for both sounds, and therefore we must assume that the divergence was of later origin than the invention of their alphabet. So with the ח in Hebrew and its representatives in the northern Semitic dialects. The Arabic and Ethiopic made of this letter, which had a fluctuating, uncertain character in Hebrew, two distinct unvarying sounds, for which they devised special characters, ح, خ; ሐ, ኀ. Looking at this tendency to multiplication of guttural sounds, which is so unmistakable in those languages which had the best scope for the development of their inherent capabilities — a tendency whose operations can be so easily traced; and looking, on the other hand, at the liability to the reduction of those gutturals to the simple smooth and rough breathings which we find essentially in all languages, we naturally conclude that they were all gradually developed out of those primary sounds. That this is so is reduced almost to a certainty when we attempt to utter those sounds, and find that they are all distinctly related in two orders which have as close a relation to one another as *d* bears to *t*. The Arabic ع and غ (=ע) are developed from

[1] Ayin, the most peculiar of the gutturals, seems to have had a tendency in two opposite directions after its origination, more marked than in any other of its class. The tendency to greater strength and variety we see exemplified best in Arabic. The inclination to weakness and assimilation we see in the later history of all the other dialects, while in Assyrian it is only and always a mere vowel. In the Samaritan, Galilean, and Talmudic dialects, and in the later Phenician א took the place of ע. Later Ethiopic and Mandaite retained only the smooth and rough breathings.

ן (=א), while c̣ and ċ̣ are developed from צ (=ה); the former order being just the sonants of the latter respectively. For the sounds in each order essentially the same organs are employed. The possible modifications in position may be illustrated by the use of the German *ch*, or better still by the Welsh *ch*, as compared with the ordinary *h*. The peculiarity of the Semitic pronunciation is, that it has brought out the ع with its surd ح more distinctly than any other language; though, as Dr. Merkel tells us,[1] an approach to the ع or ע is heard in German speech under certain circumstances. A more minute physiological analysis of these sounds than we can give here[2] would only confirm what we have said of the easy gradations of the Semitic gutturals, and of their development from the simple breathings.

From all this it appears not only that the variety and peculiarity of these Semitic sounds offer no bar to a comparison with other linguistic systems, but also that we have arrived at the same phonological level as that upon which the primitive Aryan breaths are found to stand. Let us look at the Aryan side of the equation for a moment. We find here that, so far as we can determine, they had only the spiritus lenis,[3] not the spiritus asper. This, however, does not prevent a final equalization of the sounds in question; for the history of speech shows how soon the *h* was developed, as phonology shows how easily it arises and falls into disuse.[4] *H* is really the surd of ˒ (=א). If the organs remain in the position which they assume upon the pronunciation of any vowel at the beginning of a word, and if then we blow

[1] C. L. Merkel's Physiologie der menschlichen Sprache (Leipzig, 1866), p. 74.

[2] The reader is referred to Max Müller's Science of Language (Am. ed.), Vol. ii. p. 148, and to the works alluded to in that chapter, particularly to those of Lepsius, Brücke, and Czermak; also to the thorough and very able work of Merkel above cited.

[3] Schleicher's Compendium d. vergl. Grammatik d. indogerm. Sprachen, 4. Auflage (Weimar, 1876), p. 11.

[4] See the sounds of Zend, Old-Italian, Greek, Old-Irish, etc., in Schleicher's Compendium; and compare the phenomena of the so-called Cockney speech, as well as the use or disuse of *h* in Modern French.

instead of breathing, or, which is the same thing, make a surd instead of a sonant sound, we shall have a light spiritus asper instead of the spiritus lenis.[1] We have no doubt that the same thing was done by the Semites as by the Aryans, and that from the fundamental smooth breathing they also differentiated their *h* sound. From these, as we have seen, the surd and sonant orders of gutturals were thereafter developed. Hence we see nothing to prevent us from regarding all the Semitic gutturals as comparable with the spiritus lenis of the Aryans, which the Greeks alone expressed by a definite sign, since they borrowed their alphabet directly from a Semitic people. Of course this can be *proved* only by adequate comparison; but we are concerned now to show that the formidable list of Semitic gutturals ought not to divert us from the attempt to institute such a comparison. From what has been said it is clear that we are not justified in receiving, with Dr. Delitzsch[2] the Aryan *gh* as the analogue of what we may call the surd or *h* order of Semitic gutturals. In the first place it is most probable that the Aryan sonant aspirates, *gh, dh, bh,* arose, during the remoter history of the family, from the earlier *g, d,* and *b,* just as in Sanskrit the surd aspirates *kh, th,* and *ph* arose after its separation from the main linguistic stem. In the second place, remembering that we have to compare with the spiritus asper, or the simple *h*, we find that its origin in the Aryan languages is not due exclusively, or even in any large degree, to an original *gh*. In the old Aryan tongues there were apparently two types of guttural sound; the one being conveniently represented by the Greek χ and the other by the Greek ‘. The latter sound is of various origin. It either arises independently, as often in Greek and Latin, and other idioms, or represents an original *s, y,* or *v*, as frequently in Greek, or is due to the dropping of the *g, d,*

[1] The physiological conditions of the utterance of each spiritus are given by Merkel, op. cit., pp. 72–74, who also shows in the same connection how natural the transition is from one kind of guttural to any other.

[2] Cited on p. 20.

or *b* from the original aspirates, as occurs irregularly in all the Aryan tongues, especially in the Keltic. It is never due directly, in our opinion, to an original *gh*. *Gh*, it is true, is represented in Latin at the beginning of a root by *h*, as it is in Greek by χ; but this *h* was originally a rough guttural[1] like the Greek, and the sound was heard along with the ordinary *h* in common speech, as it was in Anglo-Saxon,[2] and other old Teutonic languages, until the latter sound took its place entirely. Further, the rough Roman *h*, as well as the Greek χ, must, we think, have passed through a stage in which it had the *kh* sound.[3] But it may be asked how the Sanskrit *h* arose. It represents mostly an original *gh*, and is manifestly a corruption of it. It is a sonant, and is the only *h* in the Aryan tongues that is not surd. It was evidently, therefore, not primarily formed from the other aspirates through the dropping of their first element; if so it would have been a surd, as the *h* so arising became in the other Aryan languages. Its pronunciation probably somewhat resembled that of the German *g* in *Tage*, though it is not safe to speak with authority on such an obscure matter.[4] This theory would best agree with its development from *gh*. Here, then, we admit, is a guttural breath derived from *gh*. May it not have been so also with the Semitic family, if we allow it to have had at one time the *gh* sound? Certainly not; for its modifications would have brought it into range with the sonant or א order of gutturals, whereas Dr. Delitzsch makes the *gh* the Aryan representative of the ה, or surd order. Moreover, it stands most nearly related phonologi-

---

[1] Corssen : Ueber Aussprache Betonung u. Vocalismus d. Lateinischen Sprache (Leipzig, 1868), Vol. i. pp. 96, 97.

[2] March's Anglo-Saxon Grammar, p. 17.

[3] The Keltic (Old Irish) *ch* is corrupted from *c* (*k*), occasionally from *g*; Zeuss, Grammatica Celtica, 2d ed. (Berlin, 1871), pp. 63-71, comp. pp. 74, 78; Schleicher's Compendium (4th ed.), pp. 273-279. The Aryan *gh* becomes *g* in Keltic.

[4] Schleicher (Compendium, 4th ed., p. 17), gives it the sound of the German *h*, made sonant. Bopp (Kritische Gramm. d. Sanskrita-Sprache, 4th ed., p. 20 f.), makes it equal to the Greek χ softened. This agrees more nearly with our own view, and harmonizes better with our theory as to the genesis of each sound.

cally to ع, the Semitic guttural;[1] which, as we have seen, was not the first, but the very last of the Semitic gutturals in the order of development.

We have dealt thus at length with the guttural sounds, because they are so numerous and so peculiarly Semitic, and seem to present obstacles in the way of a comparison with the Aryan family which the other classes of sounds do not. The conclusion at which we arrive is, that all of these gutturals in our comparisons ought to be disregarded, as they are of purely Semitic development. The spiritus lenis, ‑' or א, is all that was common to Aryan and Semitic at the time of their separation, if they ever spoke a common idiom at all.

It is impossible for us to write, in this connection, at the same length of the other classes of comparable Aryan and Semitic sounds. The same principles which were maintained with regard to the development of the variant gutturals will hold with regard to the differentiation of other sounds within the bounds of their own generic classes. We shall therefore proceed more rapidly to an examination of the remaining contents of the Aryan and Semitic alphabets.

Next to be considered are the other weak sounds v (w) and y. As far as can be made out at the present stage of linguistic science, these were radical sounds in the two great families, though their history has been strikingly different in many respects. As to the Aryan v, the fact admits of no question; as to the y, though it does not occur in many Aryan roots, yet these are very ancient, and its use both in the pronouns and in inflective elements shows that it could not very well have been developed from an original i, from which it often arises in both Aryan and non-Aryan linguistic forms. It is to be noted, however, that in roots, not in formative elements, the use of v preponderates largely over that of y. The same holds true in the Semitic family. Y is much more rarely found in the triliteral roots than is v.

[1] It has been observed by Sweet that the German g in *Tage*, or the Modern Greek γ sometimes passes into a uvular r; this is the vanishing sound of the Arabic letter.

What is most remarkable, however, about these sounds, from a comparative point of view, is that they are vastly more numerous in roots of the Semitic family than in those of the Aryan. This is certainly a most instructive fact, as it is one that cannot be ignored in any just investigation of the general question of Aryo-Semitic relations. It may be accounted for in this way: Over and above the normal representatives of the Aryan *y* and *w* in Semitic, there would be two occasions of a large addition. First, it is natural to assume that these primary vowels of the Aryo-Semitic stock would often harden into semi-vowels; *i* and *u* would thus become *y* and *v*, in a consonantal system like the Semitic. Again, in many of the originally biliteral roots in Semitic, these would become triliteral through the use of weak letters such as *y* and *v*. Hence a Semitic *w* or *y* would in comparisons have to be regarded sometimes as having no representative in the Aryan speech, sometimes as representing an Aryan *u* or *i*, and sometimes their own phonetic equivalent. It is scarcely necessary to say that the Semitic forms in which either of these sounds occurs require great delicacy and caution in treatment; for we must not only ascertain to what class each belongs as regards its origin, but also to discriminate carefully between the two letters, inasmuch as they so frequently interchange, especially in some of the dialects. On these sounds we have nothing further to remark, except to say that, according to our present light, Dr. Delitzsch appears to be fully justified in excluding the Aryan *y* from his table of phonetic correspondences.

The sounds *l* and *r* come up next for discussion. Dr. Delitzsch, in his table above cited, makes the Aryan *r* representative of the Semitic *r* and *l*. We have no objection to this statement; but it requires to be properly explained, from a consideration of the true relations of the two sounds to one another. First, as to the Aryan sounds. It is usually held, mostly through the influence of Schleicher [1] and Fick,[2]

---

[1] Compendium, etc., pp. 11, 162.
[2] This is assumed throughout his Vergl. Wörterbuch d. indogerm. Sprachen.

62   RELATIONS OF THE ARYAN AND SEMITIC LANGUAGES.

that the primitive Aryan had no *l*, and that in all the cases of the appearance of that sound in the diverging languages, it arose from the *r*. This is one of the most interesting questions in Aryan phonology, though one which cannot be discussed here. We only remark upon it that the contrary opinion, which has been defended by Heymann,[1] seems to be entitled to at least as much support.[2] With regard to the Semitic *l* and *r* the sources of evidence are still fewer and more doubtful. But as to both families we would maintain that both sounds once existed, though vaguely and even interchangeably pronounced. In behalf of this we would cite the history of the sounds in all families that possess them. There are no sounds in human speech more liable to confusion and interconversion.[3] Even in the Aryan tongues, where as a rule *l* is developed from *r*, the change from *r* to *l* is not infrequent.[4] In the Dravidian family of languages, the Tamil, Telugu, Canarese, etc., *r* also changes into *l*, though the reverse is very often the case.[5] In some of the dialects of Polynesia, of South Africa, and of the Indians of North America the confusion is almost universal.[6] In some words the speaker is heard to pronounce *l*, and in other words *r*, when the sound is radically the same. In some languages the *l* is wanting, as in Zend, as also in old Persian,[7] in Ar-

[1] Das *l* der indogermanischen Sprachen gehört der indogerm. Grundsprache (Göttingen, 1873).

[2] A full review of the controversy and of the state of the question is given in Pezzi's Glottologia aria recentissima, pp. 17–24. The author himself holds to to the belief that *l* was a primitive Aryan sound.

[3] Even cultivated persons speaking highly developed languages are liable to this infirmity, e.g. Alcibiades who was ridiculed by Aristophanes for his use of *l* for *r*, Vespae 44. Cf. Plutarch, Vit. Alc. 1. This was probably not affectation.

[4] See some examples in M. Müller's Science of Language (Am. ed.), ii. p. 184.

[5] Rev. Dr. Caldwell, Comp. Grammar of the Dravidian Languages, p. 120, cited by M. Müller, ii. p. 185.

[6] Even among the dialects which are generally supposed to have no *r* sound at all, and whose speakers are thought to use *l* in place of it in trying to utter a foreign word, cases are not unknown of the utterance of the *r*. The writer has had as a guide on angling excursions a Micmac Indian, — a tribe usually thought incapable of the *r*, — who actually changed a foreign *l* into an *r* more frequently than the reverse, saying *ricker*, for example, instead of *liquor*.

[7] Zeitschrift d. deutschen morgenl. Gesellschaft, Vols. xiii. p. 379; xvi. p. 11.

menian;[1] and in several dialects of Japan, of Africa, and America.[2] *R*, again, is wanting in Chinese, in many dialects of America and Polynesia, and in the Kafir language.[3] Some languages, again, have two *r*'s, as the dialects of Australia;[4] while others have two *l*'s, as some of the Siberian idioms.[5] One tribe, at least, of the last-named family, the Tchuktches, have two *r*'s and two *l*'s.[6] It is only necessary to add that in the literary period of the Semitic languages *r* sometimes becomes *l*,[7] though the reverse is not yet proved. From all this it seems clear that in all languages both sounds were originally one, and that, in most cases, a sound vibrating between the two. In most languages as they advanced in age the two were clearly discriminated. In the Aryan, for some time before the divergence of its dialects, they were probably not yet perfectly distinct.[8] In Semitic they must have been divaricated very early in its separate history. It follows, accordingly, that for purposes of comparison *r* and *l* in both families may be regarded as representing the same primitive sound. To the hypothetical Aryo-Semitic speech one might then justly apply the remark made by Dr. Bleek of the Setchuana dialects: "One is justified to consider *r* in these dialects as a sort of floating letter, and rather intermediate between *l* and *r* than a decided *r* sound."[9]

M and *n* do not require much discussion for the settlement of their relations in the two systems. Unlike the last two

[1] Zeitschrift d. deutschen Morgenl. Gesellschaft, Vol. xiii p. 380.
[2] Ibid., Vol. xii. p. 453.
[3] See the references in Max Müller's Science of Language, ii. pp. 179, 180.
[4] Friedrich Müller, Grundriss d. Sprachwissenschaft, ii. Band, 1. Abth. (Wien, 1879), pp. 1, 81, etc.
[5] F. Müller, op. c. p. 100.
[6] F. Müller, op. c. p. 134.
[7] So אַלְמְנוֹת Ezek. xix. 7; Isa. xiii. 22, for אַרְמְנוֹת, palaces: הַצְהִיל Ps. cv. 15 for הַצְהִיר, to make to shine (comp. Ewald, Ausf. hebr. Lehrbuch, 8th ed., 1870, § 51 c.). In Assyrian even a sibilant generally becomes *l* before a dental (Sayce, Comp. Assyr. Grammar, p. 30), but it must first have become *r*; hence the name Chaldaeans, as compared with כַּשְׂדִּים.
[8] Comp. Pezzi, Glottologia aria recentissima, p. 24.
[9] The Library of His Excellency Sir George Grey; Philology (Capetown, 1858), Vol. i. p. 135, quoted by M. Müller, Science of Language, ii. p. 184.

sounds, they are totally distinct in their origin in all languages. As nasals they are liable to occasional interchange in both families, but are not regularly inter-convertible. In the Semitic roots care must be taken to distinguish between the undoubtedly radical *n* and the same sound where it seems, upon evidence which we shall adduce hereafter, to have been used as a mere determinative, as it appears to be one of the letters most frequently employed for the purpose. Moreover, being next in weakness to *y* and *v*, it is liable to take the place of other liquid letters, as well as to interchange with *y*, a matter of very frequent occurrence. *M*, on the other hand, is much more stable than *n*. It passes into *n* much less frequently than the reverse occurs, and very rarely takes the place of the other liquids.[1] Of course, in Semitic the *m* is liable to interchange with the other labials — a phenomenon appearing in all languages possessing these sounds.[2] The Semitic *m* and *n* may be provisionally taken to represent the corresponding Aryan sounds, with important restrictions which may operate in consideration of the foregoing cautions.

We pass now to the sibilants of the respective systems. At first sight, a comparison seems very difficult, if not impossible. In the primitive Aryan there was only one *s*, the ordinary fundamental sibilant. In the Semitic idiom there are several, and it will be necessary to examine them, to classify them, and to reduce them, if possible, to their fundamental primitive sounds, so that we may get a proper basis of comparison with the Aryan *s*.

A careful comparison of the Semitic sibilants leads us to the conclusion that before the breaking up of the family there were developed four distinct sounds, answering respectively to ס, שׁ, ז, צ. These sounds emerge on comparing all the dialects,— Arabic, Ethiopic, Aramaic, Hebrew, and Assyrian,

---

[1] A rare instance of *m* arising from *l* is shown in the Arabic جُمْجُمَة *skull*, answering to the Hebrew גֻּלְגֹּלֶת.

[2] That is, nearly all known languages. In a few they are wanting altogether, as in those of the Six Nations and the Hurons in North America; in others some of them are absent, as in a few of the dialects of Africa, and throughout Australia.

RELATIONS OF THE ARYAN AND SEMITIC LANGUAGES. 65

with their subordinate varieties,— and to them all the other sibilant modifications may be reduced. The z sound (pronounced as in English) is the sonant of the surd s, and arises from it normally in all languages which possess it, though also occasionally springing from other sounds. Hence we have to account for the sounds ס, שׁ, and ץ. These conclusions we shall try to make clear.

In the first place, the s and sh sounds (Heb. ס, שׁ, and שׂ, Syr. ܣ and ܫ, Arabic س and ش, Ethiopic ሰ and ሠ, Assyrian s' and s[1]) sprang from the same source. This might be argued from the history of the sounds in languages generally, in which sh is developed from s. But we have other evidence, drawn from the phenomena exhibited by these sounds in the history of the different Semitic idioms. The distinction between the שׁ and שׂ sounds, by which the former approximated to the sound of ס[2] was made in Hebrew alone sufficiently important to be represented by a special sign. Leaving these aside, as of clearly late origin, we find that the s and sh sounds have fluctuated and varied greatly from the time of the separation of the different branches of the family. If these dialects be divided roughly into Northern and Southern Semitic,— the former including Hebrew, Aramaic, and Assyrian, the latter, Arabic and Ethiopic,— it will be found that the sh sound of the northern division is represented mostly by the s sound in the southern, while the s of the former corresponds radically for the most part to the sh of the latter. Yet the correspondence is not sufficiently regular to make this a fixed principle of sound-shifting; nor can the division given above be regarded as anything more than a very general classification. A multitude of facts could be adduced, in addition to the above, if space permitted, to show how these

[1] S' = Heb. ס, and s = שׁ. This is the usual method of transcription. It is one of our misfortunes that sh seems to represent a double instead of a single sound.

[2] That ס and שׂ were originally distinct in Hebrew is proved by the fact that the ס is represented in Arabic by س more frequently than by ش, while the שׂ is represented only by ش. See Ewald, Ausf. hebr. Lehrbuch (8th ed., 1870), § 50 a. In later times ס and שׂ were much interchanged.

sibilants varied and interchanged from the earliest known Semitic times, and that too according to no stable law of permutation, but according to local and tribal peculiarities, such as has made the *sh* sound difficult to the Ephraimites,[1] and to many others throughout the world, the same *sh* sound disappear in the later Ethiopic,[2] to a great extent in Keltic,[3] and in various other idioms. The conclusion is that the supposition of a development of *s* and *sh* from two fundamentally distinct sounds, — a notion improbable on general principles, — is untenable also on historical grounds. What the original sound was, it is impossible to determine with exactness. Most probably, however, as we shall see presently, it was that of the Hebrew ס, or the ordinary *s*, with a slight tendency to palatization which would account for the frequency of the *sh* sound in the southern dialects, and its preponderance in the northern, where other influences were also brought to bear, tending the same way.

The *z* sound (Heb. ז) arose sometimes from *s* and sometimes from the sound represented by the Hebrew ץ. In either case, as we shall see, the primary source was probably the same. It clearly was not an original Semitic, as also it was not an Aryan, sound.

It remains, then, to account for ץ and its representatives in the other dialects. This is peculiarly Semitic, running through all the branches of the family. Yet is only peculiarly Semitic as a constant letter; for the sound itself is probably heard in every language possessing sibilants at all. In English, for example, we come near it in saying *cost*, as distinguished from the *s* in *cast*. It is due there to the vowel sound with which it is connected; but in the Semitic languages its sound is the same no matter what may be the accompanying vowels. In the northern Semitic there seems to have been a slight hardening of the first part of the utterance, with almost a

[1] Judg. xii. 6.
[2] See Dillmann, Aethiop. Grammatik, p. 51. His whole discussion of the Ethiopic sibilants is very instructive, and confirms very strongly the view here advocated.
[3] Schleicher, op. cit., p. 275. Zeuss. op. cit., p. 119 f. et al.

complete closing of the organs, giving the effect of a slight
t sound before the sibilant. But even this sound was usually
transcribed by ς in the Septuagint, as Σαβαώθ for צבאות, and
very seldom by ζ. The pronunciation primarily was evidently that of a strong *s*, made with the tongue turned back
against the roof of the mouth. It stood related to the ordinary *s* as the Hebrew ט to ר. Various lines of evidence
point to the conclusion that it was not an original sound, but
one developed from the primitive *s*. First, its organic association with the latter. The original *s* was probably, as we
have seen, pronounced indistinctly, and perhaps somewhat
variously. There was that tendency among the Semites to
multiply consonantal sounds which we have already discussed. What more natural than to take the occasional sound
of *s*, just described as existing in English and elsewhere,
and make it a fixed one, without regard to the vowels accompanying, especially when it is considered that the vowels
played a secondary part, and were necessarily varied continually within the same invariable consonantal formula?
The Semites, in developing their roots, necessarily had the
sense of consonantal stability developed and continually
exercised; while the Aryans have regarded the preservation
of the vowels as essentially bound up in vital union with the
consonants. The Semites, then, would be inclined to hold
fast to each distinct consonantal sound when once made
familiar to their ears. The Aryans could not; for the same
vowels being retained in each utterance would prevent the
discrimination of the consonantal variations, just as we are
still ordinarily unconscious that the *s* in *cast* and the *s* in
cost are different sounds. Secondly, the same thing is
illustrated in the history of the most fully developed Semitic
dialects, — the Ethiopic and especially the Arabic, — where
the tendency, having once fairly set in, was carried so far
that not only the simple *s* and *t*, but also the *d* and the *z*,
had their secondary sounds. It is fair to argue, within certain well-considered limits, from the living facts of a language to its inherent tendencies, and in these later develop-

ments of the Semitic idiom we see exemplified the principles of its primitive working. In the third place, the צ sound seems not to have been originally a distinct sibilant, for it interchanges with the *s* and *z* sounds so frequently in kindred roots that we can hardly attribute the coincidences to the confusion of the sounds. One must have developed from another. For proof of this statement we must appeal to the lexicons, since we cannot afford the space needed for an adequate exhibition.

It is now proper to show how all the Semitic sibilants may be classified as to their immediate origin. To the Hebrew צ and its equivalent in Aramaic and Assyrian answer the Ethiopic አ and ፀ and the Arabic ص, ض, and ط. These were all developed at first from the צ sound, though on account of their similarity to other sounds, such as those of ת and ס, they were often interchanged with the latter, and more rarely with other sounds. According to the modern Arabic pronunciation, which may be taken as sufficiently near the ancient for our purpose, there were thus two orders of sounds; the one uttered with the tongue close to the teeth: ס, שׁ (שׂ), ז, or their equivalents; and the other with the tongue turned back against the roof of the mouth: ص (צ), ض[1], and ط.[2] In these groups ס and צ represent the primary sounds of their respective ranks. The historical development is probably to be represented by the order of the letters as they here stand, except that ז, in all likelihood, arose later than צ. While all of these were thus primarily developed from one sound, it ought to be observed that sometimes we find a sibilant degenerated from a mute, as שׁ from ת, ז from ד. In comparisons these must, of course, be carefully distinguished from those which are unquestionably of sibilant origin.

The last group of consonants to be considered are the

[1] Pronounced as *d* would be in the emphatic English syllable *odd*. The original sibilation was gradually lost. In Ethiopic it was resumed again. See Dillmann's Grammar, p. 52.

[2] Pronounced as *z* in the combination *ozz*.

so-called mutes or explosives, represented in English by k, g; t, d; p, b. Looking first at the Aryan alphabet, we find that it had, besides the primary, also a secondary [1] series of gutturals, most probably developed from the former. The sonants were also aspirated so as to yield three additional letters, gh, dh, and bh. That these latter arose later than g, d, and b we have already hinted in treating of the supposed correspondence between gh and the Semitic gutturals. This is a question which is, of course, not to be solved through accessible historical evidence. The sonant aspirates were very important and well-established phonetic elements when the several Aryan dialects branched off, and are represented more or less in them all. To show that the unaspirated sounds preceded them in origin, we shall point, first, to the fact that the aspirating tendency was evidently still present at the Aryan dispersion. The surd mutes k, t, p, were then unaspirated. They assumed the aspiration afterwards, not only in Sanskrit, but also in other Aryan dialects. But it may be said that the roots in which these aspirates are found are more numerous than those which contain unaspirated letters, and therefore the former class of sounds might seem to have been the earlier. In our view this only shows the strength of the tendency to aspirate the sonant mutes, after it had once well begun. Otherwise we would be led to curious conclusions. Take the sounds b and bh, for example. Schleicher, who also thinks that the aspirates are of later origin than the simple g, d, b, asserts that he does not know of a single example which proves beyond doubt the existence of b in the old Aryan idiom as it is accessible to us. And it is certain that this sound is never found as a final in Aryan roots, while its existence at the beginning is perhaps more than doubtful. If the aspirates were also original sounds, we should thus be compelled to believe that in the Aryan system the simple b was originally unknown, though all the members of that family subsequently developed it as one of their most

[1] The two sets are generally represented by Ascoli (the discoverer) and his followers as "k^1, g^1, gh^1; k^2, g^2, gh^2." We shall follow Fick and Curtius in writing $k̦$ for k^2. It answers to the ç of Sanskrit and Zend.

important elements, and although the same idiom had from the beginning the corresponding surd *p* unaspirated — a supposition almost, if not quite, incredible according to general linguistic experience. The conclusion seems, on all grounds, inevitable, that the primary Aryan mutes were simply *k, t, p, g, d, b*.

An examination of the Semitic mutes leads to precisely the same result. At the outset we must observe that the spirant sound assumed by *b, d, g, k, p, t* after vowels, which was, perhaps, due to Aramaic influence, and is only found in that language and Hebrew, with their dialectical varieties, was of late origin. It was unknown in Arabic, Ethiopic, and apparently in Assyrian.[1] The change of *p* into *f* in Arabic, which wholly lost the former sound, cannot be surely traced to a like influence. The same is true of the Arabic *th*. Leaving out these incidental variations, and beginning with the palatals, we find that besides the ordinary *k* we have a deeper palatal, the Hebrew ק, represented throughout the whole family. It had its origin some time before the separation of the Semitic tribes, as is proved by its individuality and vitality throughout the history of Semitic speech. It was doubtless developed from the ordinary *k* sound through the same tendency that led, in the same family, to the production of the deep gutturals. Yet it had also strong affinities with the *g* sound, as is shown by the great number of cases in which they interchange, as well as by the fact that in later Semitic times it has shown a tendency to a sonant utterance, as in Babylonian[2] and in some dialects of Modern Arabic.[3] So it also interchanges, though less frequently, with the gutturals; and, in all cases of its citation in comparisons, its true relations will have to be ascertained.

Next, as to *t* and *d*. The latter sound has a variant only in Arabic and Ethiopic. This has been developed from the ע sound, as already seen; but from its resemblance to the primary *d* sound, the latter was often interchanged with it.

---

[1] Sayce, Comp. Assyrian Grammar, p. 36.   [2] Ibid., p. 30.
[3] See Merx, in the Zeitschrift d. morgenl. Ges. xxii. 273.

ט with its representatives owes its origin to the primary *t*, though it often takes the place of ץ on account of the organic association of these sounds.¹ Less frequently it stands for an original *d*. The Arabic ث arose from *s*, as is shown, among other ways, by its correspondence with the Aramaic alone, where all the other dialects have ש.

As to the labial order of mutes no difficulty occurs. The Arabic ف is, of course, only the primary *p* become a spirant. It corresponds regularly with the *p* in the other dialects. The Ethiopic shows most peculiarity here. It has the *f* of the Arabic, and, besides the ordinary *p* (perhaps slightly assibilated) another, whose pronunciation it is difficult to discover exactly, but which seems to have been uttered quickly and emphatically, perhaps after the manner of ט as compared with ת. The two last seem to have been mostly developed from an earlier *b*, though sometimes also from *p* itself. These labials in Ethiopic are the most fluctuating sounds in the language, and have rendered their comparison with labials in the other dialects somewhat uncertain in many cases. The Semitic *b* had virtually the same pronunciation throughout the whole system. It should be added that in all the dialects not only does *b* sometimes take the place of *p*, but the other labial *m* takes the place of either. Naturally, however, this did not take place in the earliest Semitic times, and a careful examination ought to enable us, as with other cases of permutation, to determine the primary forms. This hasty survey brings us to the simple sounds *k*, *t*, *p*, *g*, *d*, *b*, as the original Semitic mutes.

We have thus reduced both the Aryan and the Semitic consonants to their primary limits. We have found that the original Aryan stock consisted of the following sounds: *k*, *t*, *p*, *g*, *d*, *b*, *s*, *r* (*l*), *m*, *n*, *y*, *v*, with the spiritus lenis. The original Semitic stock has been reduced to precisely the same sounds. No root, therefore, can be found in either

---

¹ If the tongue be very slightly moved from the roof of the mouth while the organs are in the ט position, and an emphatic hissing sound be made, the result will be ץ.

family which contains a consonant not reducible ultimately to some sound in the above catalogue.

A discussion of the vowels will not be of much importance for actual comparison, since the Semitic subordination of the vowel to the consonant precludes it generally from admission into the field of inquiry about to be entered upon. At the same time it is worth noticing that the two families show that at one time they had in common simply the primary vowels a, i, u. The recent discovery, which shows that the reputed Proto-Aryan a must be differentiated into a^1, a^2, a^3, does not invalidate the conclusion; while on the Semitic side, the fact that the Arabic and Assyrian possess just the simple scale a, i, u, proves the case for that family.[1]

As has been already suggested in connection with several of the consonants treated of above, it is not maintained that the secondary sounds were developed from the primary in every case of their occurrence in actual roots. In the foregoing discussion I have only cited the fact of such normal representation as affording evidence of the real relationship of the sounds in question. In quite a number of cases, even in Proto-Semitic, these secondary sounds, since they had been firmly established in the language, arose by degeneration from other sounds than their primary originals. The frequency with which ח appears in roots as coming from an original ק is one of many obvious illustrations of the general fact.

So much for the Proto-Aryan and Proto-Semitic sounds considered separately. The next question, as to how the sounds of the two systems represented one another in actual roots, which is one of more practical importance in the general subject, can, of course, be fully answered only when we shall have presented a comparison of the roots that may seem to claim relationship. It will be necessary, however,

---

[1] Arabic and Assyrian did not simplify the original system of vowels; the other dialects amplified it. See Schrader, in Zeitschrift d. d. morg. Gesellschaft, Vol. xxvii. p. 408.

to insert here provisionally the results of our observations as embodied in the following scheme :

Proto-Semitic.[1]				Proto-Aryan.
א ʼ,	ע ʽ			ʼ = spiritus lenis.
כ k,	ק ḳ,			k, ḳ
ג g				g (g²) gh
ת t,	ט ṭ			t
ד d				d
פ p				p
ב b				bh
שׁ s,	ס s′,	צ ṣ		s
ר r,	ל l			r (l)
מ m				m
נ n				n
ו v				v

The following remarks should be made with reference to this table.

1. In the roots that have been examined for phonetic representations, no account has been made of those which show degeneration of sound from earlier forms. The earliest historical expression of the root-idea has been taken in each instance. A fuller exhibition of later secondary sounds would otherwise have been made.

2. The absence from the above list of certain sounds that existed in one family or the other or in both is to be well noted. No root common to the two idioms containing the y sound originally has been discovered. It was noticed in the foregoing discussion that roots with y as one of their elements were not numerous in either family. Among the Proto-Semitic sounds it is to be observed that ה and ח are absent from the gutturals and ז from the sibilants. Of Proto-Aryan sounds dh is unrepresented in the hypothetical Aryo-Semitic roots. These facts lead us to suggest here that if the

---

[1] The Proto-Semitic sounds are represented by Hebrew characters; שׁ is, of course, unpointed. No satisfactory transcription has yet been devised for ע. I have adopted that most employed in Germany, which is not to be confounded with the rough breathing.

theory of the development of the secondary sounds is true, the correctness of the comparison of roots is confirmed in a remarkable manner; while, if the comparison of roots should prove to be successful, the truth of the theory of secondary sounds will have been demonstrated.

3. It will be observed that these phonetic representatives are also in most cases approximate phonetic equivalents.

In this connection it will be necessary to notice arguments that have been made against the likelihood of hypothetical Aryo-Semitic roots having preserved the same sounds until an accessible period. The form which such objections are apt to assume in the minds of scientists may be exemplified by the following citations from Professor Max Müller.[1] The remarks quoted are made in the way of caution, since, as we have already said, Professor Müller admits the possibility of an Aryo-Semitic affinity, and holds earnestly to the scientific legitimacy of the widest comparisons among the various families of speech. After speaking of the vagueness of current Semitic roots as an obstacle to just comparison, he says: " I have by no means exhausted all the influences that would naturally, nay, necessarily, have contributed towards producing the differences between the radical elements of Aryan and Semitic speech, always supposing that the two sprang originally from the same source. Even if we excluded the ravages of phonetic decay from that early period of speech, we should have to make ample allowance for the influence of dialectic variety. We know in the Aryan languages the constant play between gutturals, dentals, and labials (*quinque*, Skr. *panka*, πέντε, Aeol. πέμπε, Goth. *pimp*). We know the dialectic interchange of aspirate, media, and tenuis, which from the very beginning has imparted to the principal channels of Aryan speech their individual character (τρεῖς, Goth. *threis*, High German *drei*). If this, or much more, could happen within the dialectic limits of one more or less settled body of speech, what must have been the chances beyond these limits?" And again; "We know that words which

[1] See Chips from a German Workshop (London, 1875), Vol. iv. p. 99-109.

have identically the same sound in Sanskrit, Greek, Latin, and German, cannot be the same words, because they would contravene those phonetic laws that made these languages to differ from each other..... The same applies, only with a hundred-fold greater force, to words in Hebrew and Sanskrit. If any triliteral root in Hebrew were to agree with a triliteral word in Sanskrit, we should feel certain at once that they are not the same, or that their similarity is purely accidental. Pronouns, numerals, and a few imitative, rather than predicative, names for father, mother, etc., may have been preserved from the earliest stage by the Aryan and Semitic speakers; but if scholars go beyond, and compare such words as Hebrew *barak*, to bless, and Latin *precari;* Hebrew *lab*, heart, and the English *liver;* Hebrew *melech,* king, and the Latin *mulcere*, to smooth, to quiet, to subdue, they are in great danger, I believe, of proving too much."

It may be said, in general, with reference to such strictures that they are invalid, because the question is not one of antecedent probability, but of direct evidence. The comparer is not bound to assume that Aryo-Semitic roots will appear with the same sounds. He makes his investigations among roots having the same primary meaning in the two families, and if he finds that a large number of such forms have the same or similar sounds then it becomes probable that they were originally the same. If it further appears that the essential part of what must have been the primitive working stock of ideas of the two systems are expressed in the same or similar sounds then the probability amounts almost to moral certainty. As was said at the opening of the first chapter, the evidence is of precisely the same kind as that which obtains in linguistic comparison generally.

It is undeniable, however, that there is some plausibility in the arguments above cited based on the analogies of dialectic changes within other spheres; and those arguments therefore require some examination. The first remark to be made is, that there seems to be a misconception of the conditions of a proper inquiry. We have nothing to do, in the actual comparison, with Hebrew roots and Sanskrit words. We only use those, along with the other Semitic and Aryan dialects, for the purpose of finding out Proto-Aryan and Proto-Semitic roots. That these are accessible, if strict scientific methods are pursued, there is no doubt. Now, when these are obtained we have, of course, still two separate languages. Supposing them, however, to have come from the same source, we cannot tell how long a time had then elapsed since they had emerged from the radical stage. A glance at the difference in flectional characteristics, and at the developement of secondary sounds would seem to show that it was considerable. That it was not necessarily very long, is probable from the consideration that the formative principle must have been very busily at work in those early days of language, and must have evolved new phenomena with great rapidity. These are the conditions with which we have to do, and not those assumed by the critic.

In the second place, the inferences from Aryan phonology are somewhat overdrawn. Still remembering that we are dealing with roots primarily and not with current words, we do not seem to see the same prevailing variation and interchanging of sounds that Professor Müller speaks of. Let any one take a comparative phonological table of the Aryan languages, — such, for example, as that given in Curtius's Grundzüge, — and he will probably be struck with the general correspondences rather than with the variations. There does not appear to be a " constant play " between gutturals, dentals, and labials, such as the somewhat exceptional and still puzzling words for five would seem to indicate. Moreover, it does not seem quite just to include the Teutonic languages with the others as the best representative of Aryan phonology. Taking Sanskrit, Greek, and Latin, and with them any form of Aryan speech that is not Teutonic, it is certain that roots (if not words) occurring among them which have identically the same sound and meaning must be the same roots. Sound-shifting in the mutes is not a regular, but rather an exceptional, sort of phonetic change in the

Aryan tongues, and in the languages of the world at large. The vast development of the Teutonic family and its influence on history and civilization have given its dialects greater prominence among the Aryan idioms. Grimm's law has also assumed a large space in linguistic discussion, on account of its intrinsic interest and importance in the science of phonology. But its relative scope within the Aryan sphere does not entitle us to assign it the same importance in general questions of comparative etymology. The languages which have remained nearest to the Proto-Aryan type are free from the regular operation of this principle; and there is no evidence whatever for the assumption that the Semitic family was ever subject to its influence. On the whole, therefore, and apart from the evidence of actual comparison of roots, there is no reason for believing that the Aryans and Semites had varied their fundamental sounds radically at the period represented by the earliest accessible forms. We have seen that secondary sounds were developed and have shown how they may be reduced to their primaries.

In the third place, it is noticeable that a concession is made in the above criticisms which annuls their whole force. When it is said that "pronouns, numerals, and a few imitative rather than predicative names for father, mother, etc. have been preserved from the earliest stage," the question arises, How do we know this? What is the test? Obviously only phonetic correspondence. But how is phonetic correspondence possible among these groups of words if radical changes of sound had inevitably occurred throughout the two systems of speech? There is no escape from the force of this counter-criticism, which is applicable not only to Professor Müller, but to a large number of other glottologists, some of whom are much less favorable than he to the legitimacy of such investigations as the present. The writer may say here that, for his own part, he not only regards as ridiculous the comparisons cited at the close of the foregoing extract, but also does not think very highly even of the evidence drawn from pronouns, numerals, etc.

In connection with the table of phonetic representation above presented, this subject will be closed with the following recapitulation:

At the time of the breaking up of the Aryan family it possessed the following stock of consonants: ' (light guttural breath), k, $\underset{\cdot}{k}$, g, gh, g^2, gh^2, t, d, dh, p, bh, s, $r\ (l)$, m, n, y, v. Of these the following sounds are represented in hypothetical Aryo-Semitic remains : ', k, $\underset{\cdot}{k}$, g, gh, g^2,[1] t, d, p, bh, s, $r\ (l)$, m, n, v.

At the time of the breaking of the Semitic family, it possessed the following stock of consonants: א, ה, ע, ח, כ, ק, ג, ת, ט, ד, פ, ב, שׁ, ס, צ, ז, ר, ל, מ, נ, י, ו (=', h, ‘, h, k, $\underset{\cdot}{k}$, g, t, $\underset{\cdot}{t}$, d, p, b, s, s', $ṣ$, z, r, l, m, n, y, v). Of these the following are represented in hypothetical Aryo-Semitic remains: א, ע, כ, ק, ג, ת, ט, ד, פ, ב, שׁ, ס, צ, ל, ר, מ, נ, ו.

[1] In comparison it will not be necessary to distinguish g^2 and g.

CHAPTER IV.

MORPHOLOGY OF ROOTS.

THE stock of sounds possessed by each of the two systems before its breaking up into dialects was given at the close of the last chapter. Any verbal forms in these languages that are to be compared must first be reduced to these simple phonetic elements. I have also stated that there were two principles which must determine the choice of comparable forms: first, the primary signification of each must be shown to be the same; secondly, each term to be compared must be reduced to the form it possessed before the system of speech containing it (Proto-Semitic or Proto-Aryan) became broken up into different dialects. Keeping these principles in view, we have to proceed to an analysis and comparison of the words in the two systems that seem worthy hypothetically of such treatment. It will be necessary, however, to begin the investigation by showing how we are to deal with the living elements of language, whose seemingly endless diversity would appear to forbid any attempt to harmonize them. In both districts of speech, and especially in the Semitic, we seem to be wandering about in a vast wilderness, through which the explorer moves in a hopeless entanglement of bewilderment and confusion, never reaching a meeting-place for the paths that either lead no-whither, or cross one another perpetually, without beginning and without end. It will be needful to show that some central elevation may be gained from which we may look down upon this " mighty maze," and see that it is "not without a plan"; from which we shall be able to see that the paths which are interrupted by so many obstacles, interposed by the careless ages, still keep on their course, whether converging or diverging, and run from side to side of the great wilderness. In plainer language, it will be incumbent on us, knowing how the current terms of each idiom may be referred to their proper stems, and further to their conventional so-called roots, to show according to what laws of formation the "roots" themselves may be analyzed into their simplest expressions.

A root has been well defined by Curtius as "the significant combination of sounds which remains when everything formative and accidental has been stripped away from a given word."[1] In inflectional languages, at least, such so-called roots do not appear clearly at the first showing; and the only way of arriving at them is obviously to make sure that the forms to be examined are primary and not derivative, and then by a thorough analysis of them, with a careful application, if need be, of the known phonetic laws of the language in question, to eliminate in each case the invariable significant term from the variable and unessential suffix, prefix, or infix. When this is done, however, we find that in many cases the process of analysis is not fairly complete. In both great families of speech are still left multitudes of similar roots, with similar meanings, whose relations to one another it is the duty of students to determine. In harmony with what we would naturally suspect with regard to the growth of living speech, it is found that the primitive stock of roots at the command of the earliest speakers was enlarged according to need by internal changes or external additions. The modifying or formative elements are seen to be attached with equal freedom and regularity to all these variant similar forms, showing that these forms are independent of one another. This is not the proper place for an extended exhibition of the evidence in favor of such a

[1] Grundzüge d. griechischen Etymologie (5th ed., 1879), p. 45; cf. p. 43 f., or in the English translation (4th ed. London, 1875, 1876), Vol. i. p. 58; cf. 55 f.

doctrine. We shall presently have to cite groups of words in each family that will illustrate the position here assumed. Meanwhile, it will be enough to say that a twofold distinction has to be made with regard to the forms under discussion; and that by the common consent, if not always by the verbal agreement, of leading etymologists. First, we must distinguish *secondary* from *primary* roots, or discriminate forms that seem to have been developed out of earlier ones from those which we cannot reduce to prior conditions. Secondly, we must note a difference between *absolute* and *relative* roots[1]; remembering that in many cases analysis brings us at last to forms which it is impossible to regard as the exact ultimate expression of the radical idea; since, for example, the combinations arrived at are sometimes unpronounceable, and sometimes appear in a slightly different form in different dialects of the same family. This latter distinction, however, is evidently not to be made use of practically, and must only be kept in mind as a constant warning against the temptation to fancy that we can always succeed in harmonizing the form and substance of language according to their original identity. But the principle of the existence of both primary and secondary roots is of vital importance in glottological research, and much of what we have yet to say will be simply an attempt to trace its manifestations in Aryan and Semitic speech.

We shall first deal with the current roots of the Aryan family. The discussion of this subject will be necessarily short; and the reader is referred for a full presentation of all sides of the question to what has been written by such eminent etymologists as Pott,[2] Curtius,[3] and Fick.[4] We

[1] This distinction, adopted by Curtius, was first made in these terms by Pott. Etymologische Forschungen (2d ed.), Vol. ii. p. 246.
[2] Etymologische Forschungen (2d ed.), Vol. ii. p. 225 ff.
[3] Op. cit., pp. 31-70, English translation, pp. 40-90.
[4] Vergleichendes Wörterbuch d. indogermanischen Sprachen(3d ed., 1874-76), Vol. iv. pp. 1-120. This acute and ingenious etymologist attempts to show at length that Indo-European ultimate roots fall under three classes: 1. those which consist of a more vowel (a, i, u); 2. those formed of the vowel $a + $ a

shall give here the principles which seem to be most surely established with regard to the verbal or predicative roots. Those who are familiar with the late ingenious theorizing on the subject will see that we hold a position as conservative as is possible to any one not belonging to that obstructive sect of glottologists who refuse to analyze the current roots of any system of speech on the ground that there was no development within that sphere of language.

In analyzing the Indo-European roots we must have regard to a distinction which divides them into two great classes. We must distinguish between those forms in which new elements have been added to the old, and those in which the old have been simply modified. Both of these processes of change or development were energetically carried on, after the breaking up of the Aryan household, in every branch of the family; but their operation may also be traced more or less clearly within that stock of root-forms which was the linguistic property of all in common.

First, as to the development of new roots through modification of the old, without addition. Here we have independent Indo-European roots arising,

(1) Through the modification of a vowel in the original form. Thus the vowel *a* interchanges with *i*, as in the root *dik*, to show, as compared with *dak* (represented in διδάσκω and Lat. *doceo*); in *di*, to divide, and *da*; *pi*, to drink, and *pa*.

consonant (as *ad, ap, as*); 3. those made up of a consonant or double consonant + the vowel *a* (*da, pa, sa, sta, spa, sna*). We have space for only two or three brief criticisms of this theory. First, to be formally accurate, classes one and three ought to be brought together. No root, and, in fact, no independent articulate sound can consist of a vowel alone; the spiritus lenis preceding the vowel sound is a consonant. Second, the universal elimination of *i* and *u* from classes two and three does not seem justified by the examples given. There are some roots in which these sounds cannot be shown to be secondary; e.g. in *di* to hasten, *pri* to love, *di* to shine, the *i* cannot easily be reduced to *a*; nor can a like origin be found for the *u* in *su* to beget, *bhu* to be, *ru* (*lu*) to separate, or *yu* to join. Third, there are many cases in which a vowel cannot be shown to have been the original closing sound; thus, *mar* to rub, grind, in which the notion of physical action is inherent, is probably not developed, as Fick claims, from *ma*, to diminish; nor can an earlier vowel-ending root be well found for *vas* (*us*) to burn, *spak* to see, *bhar* to bear, *vid* to know, *yag* to honor.

Less frequently, but as clearly, *a* is obscured into *u*, as in *mud*, to be lively, compared with *mad*; *bhag*, to enjoy, share in (*fungor*), as related to *bhug* (ἔ-φαγ-ον).

(2) Through the intensification or strengthening of a vowel sound. To this influence, and not to the introduction of a new vocal element, we must ascribe such developments as that of *div* (*dyu*), to shine, from *du*, to burn (δαίω for δαϜ-ίω).; and *siv*, to sew, from *su*.

(3) Through the transposition of sounds. The only cases in which this has probably occurred are a few in which *r* is one of the sounds; thus *arg*, to be bright, has become *rag*, to color; and *arbh* (ἀλφ-αίνῳ), to obtain, has changed into *rabh* (λαμβ-άνω), to take hold of.

In class first we cannot appeal with confidence to established laws of phonetic change, if we wish to determine, in any given case, which of the double or multiple forms is the earliest.

Secondly, we must consider those roots which differ from similar ones by the possession of additional elements.

(1) We find the additional factor at the beginning of the form. The only sound that seems to play this part in the Indo-European is *s*. Its occurrence there is limited to a few cases; though in the subsequent divided life of its several dialects such a use or disuse of *s* became much more common. The root *nu*, to float, is clearly Proto-Aryan; but so also is the kindred *snu*. The root *stan*, to sound, was also heard along with the related *tan*, to stretch, just as στόνος is found in Greek in company with τόνος.

There seems to be no good reason to suppose that new Indo-European roots were ever developed by the infixing of a new sound in the old. The only sound for which such a function can be claimed plausibly is *n*. But if we examine all the forms in which this additional sound occurs, it will be found that the two hypothetical roots are not used independently of one another to form separate verbal and nominal stems, but occur side by side as the basis of derivatives that evidently spring from the same source. They are thus shown to be variations of one another, rather than distinct roots with a separate range of development and an appreciable difference of meaning. Thus the root *agh*, to press, compress, is evidently the same as *angh;* for while the former appears in the nearest Sanskrit derivative, *agha*, oppressing, evil, or as substantive, affliction, sin, as well as in the hometymous [1] words ἄχος, grief; ἔχις (= constrictor, the Sanskrit *ahi*), serpent, and the Sanskrit *ahu*, narrow, the latter is as evident in the corresponding Sanskrit, *aṅhas*, affliction, sin; the Latin *anguis*, serpent, as well as in *angustus*, narrow, and the German *eng; angor, anxius*, and the Germ. *angst*. This we give as a fair specimen of the whole class, and accordingly assume for the Indo-European system, that the insertion of an *n* sound is nothing more than the nasalization of the preceding vowel, rather accidental than essential to the autonomy of the root. It is, perhaps, a phenomenon similar in origin to the epithetic ν in Greek (ἔλεγεν < ἔλεγε), the nunnation in Arabic, and the mimmation in Assyrian, and does not correspond to an additional etymological element. On the other hand, it is probable that in many cases the *n* was heard in the original root, and the form containing it would have to be regarded as the earlier one, from which the other arose through the weakening of the sound by denasalization, till it disappeared entirely in some of the forms; though within the Indo-European sphere this process gave rise to no new roots, in the strict sense of this term.[2]

[1] This much needed term, with the corresponding "hometymon," the writer owes to the invention of Mr. S. R. Winans of Princeton College, his friend and companion in philological studies.

[2] The lately developed theory of nasal vowels casts some light upon the ultimate origin of such cases as those cited above. It was first suggested by Brugman in Curtius's Studien, Vol. ix., and has since been rectified and extended by the same scholar, and by others. See the admirable statement by Maurice Bloomfield in the American Journal of Philology, Sept. 1880, p. 292 ff. The main position is that in the Aryan system there is a full set of nasal vowels, answering to *n, m,* as Skr. ṛ, ḷ answer to *r, l* in the linguals. In Proto-Aryan these are represented by ṇ, ṃ. The *n* and *m* remain consonantal before vowels, but before consonants they take the vocalized sound which is heard under like conditions in English and other languages, as in *heavenly, handsomely* (= *hevṇli, hansṃli*). In Sanskrit ṇ becomes *a* and *an*, ṃ becomes *a* and *am*. In Greek, ṇ is *a* and *αν*, ṃ is *a* and *αμ*. In Latin they regularly appear as *en* and *em;* in Gothic and High German as *un* and *um*. In Greek and Sanskrit, therefore, an original *an* or *am* may appear as a mere vowel *a* in certain inflections.

(2) We have the most important class of root-distinctions in those forms which differ from similar ones in having the additional sound at the end. These sounds, which are quite various and usually distinguishable with clearness, have been named by Curtius[1] root-determinatives. This term, which would properly indicate a radical *significant* element, we shall adopt throughout this discussion as applying to any additional sound in either family, under the guise of a prefix, infix, or suffix, which is not a mere expansion or strengthening of the root, or a mere unessential variation of a previously existing element through ordinary laws of phonetic change. The justness of this comprehensive distinction we shall show by-and-by. Here it is in order to enumerate the letters that seem to play this part at the end of Indo-European roots.

The only vowel that appears as a post-determinative in undoubted Indo-European roots is *a*, which is found in a few secondary forms, as *dhya*, to see, from *dhi*; *gna*, to know, from *gan*, (Eng., *ken*).

As to the determinative consonants, taking them in the order of the Sanskrit alphabet, we have first[2] *k*, *ḳ*, which appears to us as certain only in the roots *marḳ*, to touch, stroke, (*mulc-ere*), as compared with *mar*, to rub; *darḳ*, to see, as related to *dar*, (Sanskrit and Lithuanian); *daḳ*, to bite, as compared with *da*, to divide, tear (whence *da-nt*, *tooth*,); *bharḳ*, to shine, (φορκός, *bright*), as related to *bhar*, itself a very early development from *bha*. It appears, moreover, at the end of many lengthened onomatopoetic roots, whose etymological relations are, of course, not so clearly definable.

g appears as a determinative in *yug*, to join, as compared with *yu*; *marg*, stroke, wipe (ο-μόργ-νυμι, *milk*), as related with *mar*; *bharg*, to shine (φλέγω, *flag-ro*, *bleach*), in connection with *bhar*, and a few others. Fick, in his discussion of these points,[3] calls attention to the existence of so many

---

[1] In Kuhn's Zeitschrift für vergl. Sprachforschung, Vol. iv. 211 ff. See his Grundzüge (5th ed., 1879), p. 69; English translation (of 4th ed.), p. 89.

[2] Fick, op. cit., iv. p. 51 ff., cites a large number of supposed cases for a determinative *k*, but most of these seem to rest on no sure etymological foundation.

[3] Op. cit., iv. p. 58 ff.

roots that differ from similar forms only in having *g* instead of *k* at the end, and assumes that *g* in such cases is only a weakening of *k*. This is hardly probable. We find no such regular concurrence of *p* and *b* in secondary forms, nor of *d* and *t*; and it is not likely that *k* alone of the hard mutes would thus be softened. *g* is also an independent Indo-European sound, of at least as much radical importance as *k*. It seems best, therefore, to assume that the affinity of the ideas to be expressed, was conveyed to the ear by the employment of similar sounds.

Out of the many cases cited by Fick [1] in which *gh* is supposed to be a determinative, we can regard as well established only *dhargh* (Eng. *drag*), as related with *dhar*, to bear.

t is plainly a determinative in *kart*, to cleave, as compared with *kar* (= *skar*, *shear*); in *pat*, to rule, as related with *pa*, to protect; and, perhaps, in *pat*, to attain to (*peto*, *find*), as connected with *pa*, to obtain.

d seems to appear certainly as a determinative only in a few roots. One clear case is that of *mard*, to crush, related to *mar*. For *sad*, to sit, there appears evidence of a primary *sa*, in Sanskrit *ava-si-ta*, literally, situated, and Latin *si-tus*, *po-si-tus*, placed; *mad*, to measure, as compared with *ma*, is also probably Proto-Aryan.

dh is found as a determinative in a few well-proven cases: *kudh*, to conceal, may be compared with *ku* (*sku*), *yudh*, fight (join battle), with *yu*, to join.

Final *n* in roots appears to be often a mere nasalized vowel. We may compare *gan*, to beget, with *ga*, (as in γέ-γον-α, γε-γα-ώς); *tan*, to stretch, with *ta* (as in τα-τός, τά-σις); *man*, to measure (as in *mensus*), with *ma*.

p is one of the most common Proto-Aryan determinatives, and easily recognized in most cases. We may bring together *karp* (*kalp*) to procure, *help*, and *kar*, to make; *dap*, to divide out, and *da*, to divide; *rip* (*lip*, a-λείφ-ω) to anoint, and *ri* (*li* as in *li-nere*); *sarp*, to creep, with *sar*, to go.

b is not to be proved as an independent determinative in

[1] Op. cit. iv. p. 61 ff.

accessible forms. As we saw in our last Article, its place was taken by *bh* in current speech. This sound occurs at the end of at least two secondary forms: *gharbh*, seize (if this is the original of the Sanskrit *garbh*, *grabh*, Eng. *grab*), as connected with *ghar*; *stabh*, to support, as compared with *sta*, to stand.

m, like *n*, is a nasalized vowel in *gam*, to go, cf. *ga*; *dam*, to bind (*tame*), cf. *da*; *ram*, to delight in, cf. *ra*, as in ἔρα-μαι; *dram*, to run (δρόμος), cf. *dra* (δι-δρά-σκω), and a few others.

y and *v* are not found as determinatives, nor indeed as final sounds in Proto-Aryan. Being semi-vowels, they would not have been sufficiently distinct for this purpose. They were used often, however, in the development of special roots in different branches of the family.

r is a very common final letter in roots, but it is generally difficult to acknowledge that it is a determinative in most of the cases adduced as evidence. Such a function may perhaps be allowed to it in *tar*, to cross over, as compared with *ta*, to stretch; in *dar*, to burst or tear open (δέρω, *tear*), as related with *da*, to divide, and it appears certain in *star* (*stal*), to place firmly (Sanskrit *sthira*, firm; German *starr*, *stellen*,), as connected with *sta*, to stand.

s is an obvious determinative in a good number of instances. Thus we may associate *vaks* (English *wax*), to grow, = *vag-s*, with *vag* (*ug*), to increase (as in English *eke*; German *auch*); *dhars*, to be confident (θάρσ-ειν, *durst*), with *dhar*, to hold (*firm*); *bhas*, to shine (found in English *bare*), with *bha*.

In the foregoing discussions we have not taken account of the claim made by Pott[1] in behalf of several Proto-Aryan roots, that they are made up of older forms, with fragments of other words prefixed. Such supposed prefixes are mostly prepositions, as in *bhrag* (*bharg*), to shine, as compared with *rag* (*arg*), of the same meaning, in which the *bh* represents the prepositions *abhi*, as found in Sanskrit. Other

[1] Etymologische Forschungen (2d ed.), Vol. ii. p. 297 ff.

kinds of words are also supposed occasionally to perform the same office, as the adverb *su*, well, in *svad*, to taste (ἄνδ-άνω, ἡδύς, *sweet*), made up of *su* and *ad*, to eat. Some of the alleged instances of such combinations are very plausible, and many are not so. For full discussion of the whole subject, the reader is referred to Curtius' Grundzüge,[1] where the theory is, we think, shown to be untenable.

The results of the investigation are briefly these: 1. Of those forms which differ from others in showing an additional element, there is only one group that has this at the beginning, namely, those in which *s* appears as the added factor. 2. There is good reason to hold that no root is modified by the insertion of any letter: the infix *n* we may call a stem-determinative, rather than a root-determinative. 3. We have found the vowel *a* used as a post-determinative, and also nearly every one of the original Indo-European consonants.

If we compare the various forms in which the additional letter occurs, it will be seen that these added sounds are of different degrees of significant value, and that the same sounds are not always of equal importance in this respect. Thus the vowel *a* seems to have usually little modifying power; but *mna* (= *mana*), to think upon, remember, is clearly discriminated by it from the more general *man*. Again, the added nasals seem sometimes, like the inserted *n*, to modify stems, rather than roots; but in *dam*, to subdue, tame, we have an obvious specializing of *da*, to bind.[2] Again, the initial *s* (as in *snu*, to float, compared with *nu*), gives or takes away no apparent force, in most cases, from the shorter form; and for this reason, as well as on account of the general uncertain tenure of the *s* in various languages of the family, Fick and others choose to regard the longer form as the earlier, and so do not consider *s* as a determina-

[1] See in the fifth German edition, p. 31 ff. English translation (of 4th ed.), p. 38 ff.

[2] Fick, in his classification, to which we have been very much indebted, gives *m* and *n* a place by themselves as being of less importance than the other determinatives.

tive at all in such cases. It is impossible to prove, however, that the *s* was really dropped from the beginning of any Proto-Aryan root; and it would seem to be more in accordance with analogy in root-formation that the shorter form should have preceded. But we think we can show, in one case at least, that the *s* is a true determinative, and the shorter the more primitive form. The root *tan*, already alluded to, means to stretch. But it yields derivatives which, along with this sense, also express the notion of sounding. Thus Skr. *tâna* and Gr. τόνος mean both stretching and a *tone;* and Quintilian [1] shows us how this is possible when he uses the Latin word *tenor* (properly a sustained course) in the sense of accent or *tone*. Going a little further, we find that in Latin *ton-o* means *to thunder*, our own English word being radically the same,[2] as also does the Skr. *tan* (*tanyati*). Now we take up the root *stan* to sound, or, more specifically, to make a deep sound. This is found in the Skr. *stan* (*stanati*) ; Gr. στέν-ω, to groan, as well as in the modern German *stöhnen*. Curtius,[3] who connects the Lat. *tono* with *tan*, to stretch, hesitates to associate the latter with *stan*, to sound, against the opinion of Pott, Benfey, Corssen, Walter, and Grassmann. But the fact that the Skr. *stan* (*stanayati*) means also to thunder, as well as to groan, bringing itself alongside of *tan* in this secondary sense, seems to complete the analogy between the two roots. Thus *tan*, to stretch, came to express the idea of a sustained or resonant sound; while *stan* was specialized into the notion of a deep, heavy sound, the noise of *thunder* being equally well associated with both. In this instance, then, *s* is clearly a determinative; though, as we have seen, it is the only initial sound so used in Proto-Aryan.

The question naturally arises, in connection with this sound, as also with any of the final determinatives, Is it

[1] Inst. Orat., i. 5. 22, 26. See Harper's Latin Dictionary, s. v.

[2] Max Müller, Lectures on the Science of Language (Am. ed.), i. 364, warns us against the fancy that the word *thunder* is onomatopoetic.

[3] Grundzüge (5th ed.), p. 217.

necessary to regard any of the forms as more primitive than the others? For all we know, may not all the variant roots have arisen side by side, without reflection, each with its own special significance, according as each idea seemed to require its fitting expression? Or another position may be taken, as by Max Müller,[1] namely, that the longer forms in any group (as *mark*, *marg*, *mard*, and *mardh*) may gradually have dropped their distinctive features, leaving only the constant formula (as *mar*) to express the general notion. These points are not of so much importance in our comparative study as they might seem at first sight; for in either case, if we find the same constant formula employed to express the same idea in both Aryan and Semitic, we are entitled to use the fact for verbal comparison just as freely as a similar correspondence between Sanskrit and Greek might be employed. But the questions are worthy of the attention which our space will allow.

As to the first, it should be answered that human language is not merely a system, co-ordinate and harmonious, but also historically a growth or a development from the very beginning, even in its radical or uninflectional stage. The *hortus siccus* exhibited by Renan in his Origine du Langage, with its dead roots and withered stems, cannot fairly represent the actual state of primitive speech. No one can compare any group of roots, of similar forms and meanings, in any system of speech, without seeing that they bear upon their very face the evidence of a change in representative sounds corresponding to a change in the ideas to be represented,— unless the observer is hampered by some philosophical theory requiring him to maintain the contrary opinion.

The second theory does not deny a living progress in primitive speech, but holds to a generalizing of forms with special meanings, rather than a specializing of ideas already general. We would say that the question here is not connected with the influence of phonetic decay; it has to do with the formation of the very elements of speech. Now,

[2] Chips from a German Workshop, Vol. iv. p. 129.

experience shows that such forms arise by composition and addition in all processes that are akin to root-making. Again, as Curtius remarks,[1] the fuller forms are the later ones. The process of expansion in roots can actually be watched as we trace the growth of the different members of the family after its breaking up.[2]

Another question of some importance remains. Can we get at the significance of these determinatives? Not in all cases, nor in most. We ought to decide, however, as to what sort of significance they may bear. Curtius says[3] that if the theory of a simultaneous development of " clusters of roots " is rejected, we must assume that there was an expansion of roots by composition, in which the added elements would have to be considered as weather-worn stems. But that seems hardly necessary in all cases. In later forms, after the original creative faculty had lost its force, such would doubtless be the character of the determinatives; and in the suffix *dh*, at least, there seems to be good reason for tracing a connection with the common root *dha*. Such also may have been the origin of the determinative *p*, which forms a causative in some Sanskrit verbs, and serves to convey the same force sometimes as the final sound of a root. Still, there is nothing certain about these cases, and in most instances not even can a plausible conjecture be made. There seems, indeed, no reason to disbelieve that the earliest determinatives were themselves as primary as the roots which they modified, and that they stood as the symbols of general qualifying notions, rather than as fragments of previously existing stems. The question differs completely from that which relates to the origin of the inflective elements, for each of these latter has a definite invariable meaning. In considering root-formation in Proto-Semitic, the same conclusion appears also inevitable there; and a close study of the latter subject would, we think, be very serviceable to Indo-European

---

[1] Grundzüge (5th ed.), p. 66, note; cf. p. 69, note.
[2] Thus the root *sta* is Proto-Aryan; *stand* is Teutonic.
[3] Op. cit., p. 69, note; English trans., p. 90, note.

specialists, as tending to throw light on the workings of the mind of man in his evolution of primitive speech.

It only remains to be said, in this connection, that, as a matter of course, any true Proto-Aryan root may be used for purposes of comparison, whether it be primary or secondary. The matter is one of scientific etymology, and the only restriction to be set in the choice of comparable forms is obviously this: that any root which can be proved to have originated in any single one of the three great divisions of the family, the Indo-Eranic, Graeco-Italo-Keltic, and Slavo-Teutonic,[1] must be rigorously excluded. Thus it would be allowable to compare the root *bharg*, to break, as well as the primary *bhar*, with any Semitic form, because the former root, though perhaps not to be found in Indo-Eranic, occurs in the widely-divergent Graeco-Italic and Slavo-Teutonic, and therefore is probably Proto-Aryan. Again, not only may the primary root *bha*, to shine, be used in comparisons, but also its secondary *bhar*, and even the more fully expanded form *bharg*, of similar meaning, since all these are found in all the divisions of the family. But it would not be proper to use the Teutonic *hlad*, to lade, or *gald*, to be worth, since these are not found in any other division.

We have now to take up the subject of the morphology of Proto-Semitic roots. The problem here is the same as that presented in the Proto-Aryan, and the method of solving it the same as that just employed for the latter system. The subject, however, is one of greater difficulty and obscurity, and we shall not be able to get much light upon it from the labors of previous investigators. As this field is not so familiar to linguistic students as the Indo-European province, we shall exhibit the true process of inquiry a little more in detail.

First, of course, we have to fix the true criteria of a Proto-Semitic root. It is manifest that we must begin by showing that any such hypothetical form must be found represented in more than one branch of that family. The four great divisions we take to be the Assyrio-Babylonian,[1] the Aramaic,

[1] The writer does not deny the correctness of the more fundamental division

the Hebraic, and the Arabo-Ethiopic, with their respective dialects. A root found in Arabo-Ethiopic and any one of the other three branches, is certainly Proto-Semitic; a root found in all of the other three is probably so. Now, in ascertaining the true roots, whether primary or secondary, we must, of course, have respect only to the laws of Semitic speech. In the last Article it was shown that of the phonetic elements of that system some were certainly secondary. But it must be remembered that of these only a few modified sounds were developed after the breaking up of the family; and it is to the regular phonetic stock employed by the Semites in their common home that any hypothetical root must be referred. As a general safeguard, it should be remembered that the question before us at present is purely a Semitic one. In the analysis of roots the object must not be to try to quadrate them with the Proto-Aryan, but to see what results may be arrived at from a study of Semitic morphology alone, without regard to the phenomena, or even the existence, of any other human idiom. The fact that such investigations have usually been made in the interest of a reconciliation with the Aryan system has tended to discredit the conclusions arrived at by previous inquirers.

The first thing that strikes any one who takes a survey of the Semitic field is the remarkable fact that all the roots of that system of speech when inflected appear in a triliteral form, at least in all those dialects which have reached their highest flectional development. This phenomenon is undoubted, and expresses an undeniable tendency of the earliest speakers to make all the roots tri-consonantal, however they

---

into East and West Aryan; he only holds that the European branches represent a much larger number of the oldest dialects of the system, and therefore, for *comparative* purposes, should count for more than the Indo-Eranic alone. A like remark should be made upon the classification given of the Semitic family. There can be no doubt that the southern division, represented by Arabic proper, Himyaritic, and Ethiopic, is of far more importance as a Proto-Semitic indicator than any one of the northern languages. But there should be as little doubt that the members of the northern division, taken together, must count for more than the southern alone, in the comparison of roots. Cf. Schrader, Zeitschrift d. deutschen morg. Ges., Vol. xxvii. p. 401 ff.

may seem to have disregarded the principle in some cases, which we shall notice presently. The question at once arises: Must we hold that all these roots were tri-consonantal from the beginning, and that the apparent exceptions are only degenerated, shortened forms; or do any of the roots show peculiarities that would lead us to infer that they have developed from more elementary conditions? An affirmative answer seems due to the second alternative; and, though this is not the place for a full discussion of the matter, we shall adduce a few of the considerations that seem to point clearly to that conclusion.

First, we have the co-existence of a large number of roots of similar sound and related meanings, which differ from one another only in one of the radicals. Thus (*a*) the first two consonants of each member of the group are the same, the third being different throughout the list; or (*b*) the last two radicals of some roots may contain the constant formula, the first being the variant; or (*c*) the second letter may appear as additional, the first and third representing the essential significant combination. This would seem to show that the forms with the variant letters were developed from earlier roots represented in the present stage of the language by the two constant letters in each hometymous group.

Further, we have still more conclusive evidence from those hypothetical forms in which the third radical is the same as the second. Comparing with class (*a*), mentioned above, we find that in nearly all those groups of roots which agree with one another in the first two consonants and differ in the last, there appear forms in which the last letter is not a variant, but merely the second repeated. Moreover, such forms (giving rise to the so-called עע stems) are generally more comprehensive in meaning than the related roots with variant letters, containing the generic idea whose specific modifications are expressed by the divergent forms. These facts indicate that they represent an earlier expression of thought than the longer roots, and this is naturally obtained by dropping the repeated consonant. In other words, we infer that the early speakers developed these assumed triliterals from earlier biliterals by simply repeating the second sound. The production of the hometymous forms is thus more easily accounted for, upon any theory of phonological or morphological symbolism, than if we were to suppose that the longer forms were the earliest. In fact, the latter supposition would only accord with the theory that the Proto-Semitic language was not a growth at all, but an institution founded after solemn deliberation. In that case we would have to suppose that the primitive Semites, in convention assembled, passed a resolution to the effect that no one should frame and pronounce a word having a root of either more or less than three legal consonants. For we must remember that these forms are evidently a part of the very oldest stock of roots in the whole system; and unless we assume a phonological miracle, it is impossible to believe that such an elaborate and consistent complexity of sounds could be the first expression of Semitic thought, especially when the combination looks so much like a mere prolongation or repetition of simpler elements.

Again, it must not be overlooked that the Semites disliked the close repetition of the same sounds rather more than other peoples did; and we can best account for their toleration of such phenomena, either before or after the family separation, by assuming that, in order to conform to the triliteralism which the increasing demand for adequate expression had gradually been developing, they first doubled the second letter in certain biliteral roots, and then in certain inflections and derivatives from the same roots sounded that letter a second time.[1]

In this discussion we have adopted the current terminology of these roots, as though the second radical were actually repeated in the ultimate basis of noun and verb stems. But it is really doubtful whether in Proto-Semitic such a repeti-

[1] On the question whether the doubled or the repeated forms were the earlier, see the just remarks of Stade, Lehrbuch d. hebräischen Grammatik (Leipzig, 1879), § 143 a.

tion occurred at all. The Assyrian, otherwise not highly developed among the Semitic languages, is the only member of the family that makes them in the verb-stems consistently triliteral, while in none of the dialects are shortened forms given up in the noun-stems. Moreover, there are certain of the inflections which seem to show that a third radical did not primarily exist. Otherwise, it is hard to explain such a form as the imperfect יִקֹּר in Hebrew. If the root were really קדד, the third radical, not being weak, would have to be retained or represented. We must, then, regard such עע roots as real biliterals in Proto-Semitic. Accordingly, whether we apply to the subject inductive or deductive arguments, the result is the same. Thus a large class of current Semitic roots yields to analysis, and the principle of triliteralism is shown not to be inviolable.

Still further, we have the evidence afforded by the so-called עי and עו verbs. The close relation between these and the class just discussed has always been observed, and the conviction is now pretty well fixed among Semitic scholars that they have a common origin, however remote this may be. There is no doubt, however, that these roots assumed an independent form before the breaking up of the family, as they are found with a characteristic system of inflection and derivation in all the dialects. Yet here, again, the proof of triliteral origin is wanting. Of course, it is easy to say that the prevailing type of stem-formation in the Semitic generally points to a triliteral beginning here as elsewhere. It is just here, however, that the very premises of such an argument fail us. In some of the dialects the stems are not triliteral at all. In Assyrian we have the most imperfect development of these forms. The verb stems coincide in some of the conjugations with those of עע verbs (as in Hebrew, and to a less extent in Aramaic) and are even confounded in others with פי and פא forms. In Hebrew also there is no characteristic triliteral stem-formation. In all the stems we have regularly a biliteral base. The intensive stem is no exception, since it simply repeats the last radical, forming the so-called Polel (Proto-Semitic Palel), after the analogy of the עע roots. The existence of the form קָיֵם may be pointed to as rebutting our sweeping assertion. But this only confirms our general position; for it is only in later writings that such a form occurs, which would of itself be conclusive proof that the tendency was to develop triliteral forms from shorter ones, and that the current biliterals are not degenerations of longer primary forms. The designations usually given to this class of verbs call for some remark. The name עו is misleading. The true עו root is that in which the ו is a primary consonant, as in Hebrew צָוָה, and many other cases in the various dialects. The native Arabic grammarians call them concave, or hollow, roots, a term which shows how slight is the claim these forms have to be considered tri-consonantal, even in that most fully developed of Semitic tongues. The appellation, roots with a medial vowel, is hardly manageable in English. The formula עו, adopted by Stade in his Lehrbuch, is not correct, inasmuch as it assumes that $\hat{a}$ is invariably the inherent vowel. The Arabic designation seems to characterize the typical form pretty fairly, and is, perhaps, on the whole, the one to be preferred. Our view of the origin of the whole class will be given when we come to treat particularly of its formation.

Evidence, no less clear, of a development of shorter primary roots is afforded by the so-called לה stems. These undoubtedly point to a primary form similar to those which the other two classes imply; and with them, also, it is clear that the final element cannot originally have been a consonant. The most definite thing to be said about them is that the old root appears to have been expanded by the addition of a vowel, i or u, at the end, which, under certain conditions, became hardened into a semi-vowel, y or v. The phenomena of noun and verb inflection in all the dialects point to this conclusion. The assumption that the original form in each case was triconsonantal is met by a multitude of facts which it cannot be reconciled with. Take, for example, verb forms in Hebrew, Assyrian, and Aramaic, which stand here upon nearly the same level of development. It is not easy to account for the 3. fem. sing. גָּלְתָה in Hebrew, or the 3. pl. גָּלוּ, and analogous forms, on the theory of a degeneration from triliterals. But it would require even greater ingenuity to show that a like origin is to be assumed for the suffix forms of this class of verbs in Hebrew, as e.g. גָּלָם, גָּלְךָ, פְּלֵנִי. The suffix-formation is very old — Proto-Semitic in fact — and even in other dialects, where a fuller form is used before suffixes, the same reminiscence of a shorter stem is observable.[1] Of course it is not here maintained that the longer type of formation with the added vowel or semi-vowel was not developed in the Semitic family before its breaking up. On the contrary, we believe that these *quasi* triliterals are really Proto-Semitic. It is only claimed that, as we learn from forms exemplified by the preceding citations, the only satisfactory theory of their ultimate origin is the one just given.

From all that has been said, it is clear how little evidence there is for the assumption that all the Semitic roots were originally triconsonantal. The three classes known as ע"י, ע"ע, and ל"ה roots were all developed from shorter forms, according to fixed principles. Having thus secured a sure means of ascertaining the primary roots of the system, we shall now exhibit in detail, as was done with the Proto-Aryan, the various modes by which the secondary roots are developed.

First as to the development of secondary roots through predeterminatives, or the prefixing of an additional sound. According to our observation, no letter, with the exception of gutturals, is thus employed in Proto-Semitic which is not also

---

[1] For example, the Mandaite and Talmudic dialects, which in these forms agree more nearly than do the Syriac and Hebrew with the perfect verb, also show occasional instances of the use of the shorter primary stems. Prof. Nöldeke, than whom there is no higher living authority on such matters, says on this point: "Whatever theory may in general be held as to the origin of the weak roots, no doubt can be entertained that in *these* forms, the employment of the third radical as a consonant is secondary, and has been brought about through the analogy of the strong verb." — Mandäische Grammatik (Leipzig, 1875), p. 284.

a formative or inflective element of the language — a fact of the very highest importance in its bearings both upon Semitic and upon general linguistic morphology.

א[1] is a predeterminative in Proto-Semitic, as may be seen from the cases now to be cited : בר, to cut off, separate (Heb. בַּר; Arab. بَلَّ) yields אבר to be separated, to be lost, to perish (Heb. אָבַר; Aram. אֲבַר, أَصْم ; Eth. አብደ). כף to bend (Heb. and Chald. כַּף, Syr. ܟܦ, to bend; Arab. كَفَّ, to turn aside), gives us אכף, to bend for a burden (Heb. אָכַף in causative sense, cf. אֶכֶף, burden; Syr. أَكَفّ, to oppress; Arab. أَكَفَ, II. IV. to saddle). Other examples are found in אסף, to scrape up, add, accumulate, from סף, to scrape ; אסר, to bind, from סר, to press together, bind. These also may be abundantly attested as Proto-Semitic.

ה is a rare predeterminative in Proto-Semitic; nor is it a very common one in any of the dialects in their separate history. A very probable instance we take to be found in הבר, to divide up (Heb. חָבַר, ἅπ. λεγ.; Arab. هَبَرَ) from the familiar root בר to cut, divide. On the same level stands הרם, to be high (Heb. הרם, found in derivatives ; Arab. هَرَمَ, whence هَرَم, pyramid), from the widely-extended root רם. The root הלך, to go away (Heb. הָלַךְ; Aram. הֲלַךְ, هَلَكَ; Arab. هَلَكَ, to perish), furnishes another example; for though לך is not found as Proto-Semitic, it may be inferred with certainty, through a comparison of the related forms, ילך, חלך, לאך, שלך, as represented in various dialects, in all of which the notion of going is manifest.

ו is a predeterminative in the following among other cases. ירד, to go down (Arab. وَرَدَ, to go down to the water; Heb.

---

[1] The letters of the Hebrew alphabet will be used throughout to represent primary Semitic sounds and forms; as was before stated.

ירד, and Assyr. ארד[1] to descend, for the earlier וירד), proceeds from רד, to thrust, push, cause to go (Heb. רַד; Arab. رَدَّ; cf. רָדָה and رَدَى). וכל, to contain, hold, be capable (Heb. יכל, to be able; Arab. وَكَلَ, to regard as able, trust in; Assyr. אכל[1] contain, maintain), is developed from כל, to surround, enclose, contain, one of the most common and widespread of Semitic roots.

י is a predeterminative in יקץ, to awake (Heb. יָקַץ; Arab. يَقَظَ and يَقِضَ), as compared with קץ, which, though only found in Hebrew, is almost certainly Proto-Semitic. We may also compare ימן, the root of the Semitic word for the right hand, with אמן, to be firm, found in all the divisions of the family; and ישר, to be right, prosperous, with the kindred אשר, both Proto-Semitic, as being found in all the dialects. י was not employed in this way by the early Semites nearly so often as ו.

ח is probably a determinative in the Proto-Semitic חנק, to press, choke, make narrow, found in all the dialects, either in noun or verb stems. This may be connected with the equally ancient ענק, to put round the neck, if the primary notion of the latter is of close binding; while the Syr. شَنَق, Chald. שְׁנַק, Arab. شَنَقَ, to strangle, is clearly a kindred causative. Another case is perhaps the ח in Proto-Semitic חדל, to let go, cease, etc., as connected with דל, to be loose, which is developed in various forms throughout the family. חתם, to close, seal, may possibly furnish another example, but the proof would be precarious. We must acknowledge that the evidence is not conclusive for any other instance of the use of ח as a predeterminative. The persistence and independent

---

[1] According to the law discovered and established by Oppert (see his Grammaire Assyrienne, 2d ed., 1868, p. 9 f.), the Hebrew פי׳ forms usually become מאַ׳ in Assyrian, if they correspond to פי׳ in Arabic; but when the Arabic preserves the Hebrew י the Assyrian does so also. The Hebrew forms require no explanation.

RELATIONS OF THE ARYAN AND SEMITIC LANGUAGES. 101

force of this sound from the earliest Semitic times, is one of the most important facts in the phonology of the system.

מ is a predeterminative in one or two roots with a causative force. Thus משׁל, to extend, lengthen (Heb., Arab., and Targ., either in noun or verb stems), may be compared with שׁול, to be long (as in Arabic; the Heb. הֵטִיל means to throw = send along). Such developments were common enough in the several dialects in their separate history. In Ethiopic they became quite fashionable. In the primitive speech they were very rare — a fact which may perhaps go to show that מ as a servile letter was of later origin than some of the others, being a nominal, not a verbal formative.

נ was a very common Proto-Semitic predeterminative. Thus, נתן, to give (Heb., Chald., Samar.; the Assyr. נדן shows a customary softening of *t* to *d*), is plainly developed from the familiar root תן, to stretch, in the sense of reaching forth. נסך, to weave together, cover over (Heb. סָךְ; Assyr. נסך; cf. Arab. نسج), is formed from סך (Heb. and Assyr. סַךְ, to weave, to cover; Arab. شَكَّ, to cover with armor). נגר, to move along (Chald. נגר, to draw, to flow; Heb. נגר, to flow, to rush; Assyrian *nagaru* to overwhelm; and perhaps Eth. ነገረ, to speak = make words flow forth, express), is developed from גר, a common Semitic root, meaning to drag, draw along. The Arab. جَرَى, to flow, is an instructive connecting link. Many other examples might be adduced.

ע seems to be, in a few cases, a Proto-Semitic predeterminative. עקר, to cut, dig out (Heb. עָקַר, with kindred meanings in Chald. and Syr.; Arab. عَقَر, wound, etc.), is probably formed from the wide-spread primitive root קר, to cut, dig. ערך, to dispose in order, arrange together (Heb. עָרַךְ; cf. Eth. ተአረከ, III. 3, to make an alliance or friendship), cannot be separated from ארך, to stretch out (Heb., Arab., Syr., and Samar.; Talm. to arrange, prepare; for the connection of meanings, cf. the Latin *rego* with *rectus*).

ש is an occasional predeterminative in primitive Semitism. We may compare here the two roots ובל and שבל, to flow, go, which agree remarkably in Heb., Arab., Aram., and Assyr., either in the primary or secondary senses, or in both; and that with respect both to the verb and the noun stems. The root כן (כון), to be fixed, gives rise to שכן, which in Assyr. has the proper causative sense, to establish, and in the other dialects becomes reflexive or intransitive: to establish one's self, to dwell. שכב, to lie (Heb., Aram., and Ethiopic), is probably developed from the old root כב, to bend, curve (cf. *recline*). ש was much more frequently used in this way in the various dialects in their separate history, such an employment of it being specially noticeable in Assyrian.

Of the use of ת as a predeterminative, of which we find frequent examples in the later history of the dialects, we find at least one sure example in Proto-Semitism: תקן (Heb. Aram. and Arabic, to be straight, solid; cf. תכן) from the ancient root קן (cf. כן); while others are probable.

Next, we have to consider the various modes of expanding a primary root by means of internal modifications, or the use of indeterminatives.

א is an indeterminative in באר, to dig (Heb., Arab., Aram., and Assyr., in noun or verb stems), springing from the wide-spread ancient root בר, to cut, to bore. The same use is exemplified in מאר, to be large, great (in Assyr. noun and verb stem in the general sense, as also in noun-stem in Heb.; in Arab. specially of the growth of plants: cf. مَهَدَ, to spread) from the root מד, to extend, found throughout the Semitic system. We may also compare מאס, to flow, as blood from a wound (Heb., Chald., with an allied sense in Arabic), and מס, to be liquid, also unquestionably primitive. Many other examples might be adduced; and it is safe to say that in every case in which the last letter of a triconsonantal root is "strong," and the first letter primary, a medial א is determinative. Here, as elsewhere, א is used in the interest of a vowel, which is the real modifying element in this variety of root-formation.

ה is an indeterminative in נהר, to shine forth (Assyr., Aram., Heb., and Arabic, in noun or verb-stems, or in both); cf. נור, to shine, which appears likewise in all the divisions of the family. So also דהר, to revolve, keep going (in Assyr., Aram., Heb., and Arabic, either in noun or verb stems), developed from the ancient common root דר (cf. דור). In this use ה is nearly as common as א.

ו, more frequently than any other letter, represents an internal development of the root. It is, of course, demonstrable that this shows a secondary form only when we can compare with the simpler so-called עע roots. Such cases, however, are quite numerous. Thus we have גור, to turn aside, sojourn, found in all the dialects, as compared with גר, to turn, to twist, to roll, equally Proto-Semitic; דור, to revolve, as related with דר, which expresses various kinds of irregular motion in the different dialects. We may compare also ניד and נד, both primitive roots expressing rapid motion and flight; כד and כור, both Proto-Semitic, of which the former means, to arrange in a series, to number, and the latter, to repeat. Many other cases might be cited; and it may be stated as a general fact, that when we have an עי and an עע root, side by side, with the first and last letters the same in both, the radical notions in both may be easily connected. Objection might be brought on the score of the want of association between a few of such cases. The only exceptions we know of in Proto-Semitic are the roots from which spring יום, day, and ים, sea (but we have not any verb-stems from these roots, and therefore can say nothing as to the primary meanings), and חיל, to whirl, twist, which does not seem connected with חל, to pierce, to open. שוב, to return, may be explained as connected with סב, to turn around; at least, that is the only primitive root with which it can be compared.

It is now proper to give what seems to us to be the true view of the origin of these forms. It being quite certain that inflection had begun long before the roots had been universally raised to the tri-consonantal type, the matter of assimilating the shorter forms to that standard was accomplished apparently in this way. While the עִעִ roots reached this level by having the second radical emphasized or doubled (and afterwards, in certain inflections, repeated), the עִי roots entered upon the same stage by having the characteristic vowel of each stem lengthened. Thus *kam* in inflection would become *kâm*: and *kum*, *kûm*.[1] Not till a much later period did the more highly developed of the Semitic dialects, Arabic and Ethiopic, make of these stems distinct roots. From this it follows that a medial י represents merely a lengthened inflective vowel in Proto-Semitic, and not a radical sound.

ה as an ancient indeterminative can be held to be probable in only one instance that we can adduce. A plausible case is מחר, the root of מחיר, price, which it would seem proper to connect with מחר, to sell, and מיר, to exchange.[2] But it is not Proto-Semitic in that sense, only Hebrew; the Assyr. *maḥirn*, offering, tribute, which Lenormant[3] connects with מְחִיר, being derived from the native root מחר, to be in front, and in causative forms to bring before, or present.[4] A surer instance is found in סחר, to go round, traverse (Heb., Aram., and Assyr.), as compared with סהר, to be round (Heb. and Aram.; cf. Arab. شَهْر, moon, with Heb. שַׂהֲרוֹן, and Syr. ܣܗܪܐ), both of which may be connected with Heb. סור, to turn aside, from the primary notion of bending. Of course, it may be suspected that סחר may be merely a strengthened form of סהר, especially as in Assyrian the former root has the intransitive meaning attaching in the other dialects to the latter. In general, we may say of medial ה what has

---

[1] See a brief but instructive discussion of this question by Prof. A. Müller in Zeitschrift d. d. morg. Gesellschaft for 1879, p. 698 ff.

[2] Not with מָכַר to sell, which is probably a secondary, derived from כרה to buy (cf. the use of מ as a predeterminative discussed above).

[3] Étude sur quelques parties des syllabaires cunéiformes (Paris, 1876), p. 247.

[4] The conjecture of Friedr. Delitzsch (Assyr. Studien, Part i. p. 125), that the Hebrew and Assyrian roots are connected, is probably wrong.

been said already of initial ה, that it is normally an independent stable sound.

Medial י appears to represent an expansion of the root in several cases. שׂים, to place, lay down (in noun or verb stems in Heb., Aram., and Assyr.), must be compared with שׁת, which is also possibly primitive, being found in both Heb. and Aram. in the same sense. So also apparently with קין, to fashion, forge, as compared with קן, to set right, prepare.

In these י appears to be Proto-Semitic; and yet here, as well as in the many cases where 'עי and 'עו forms exist side by side in the same sense, it is very doubtful whether the י is primary. It seems more probable that it took the place of ו in these instances; it having perhaps been shortened from the causative form of the verb-stem in each case, since such 'עי stems are mostly transitive. If this view is correct, we cannot maintain that י represents a Proto-Semitic indeterminative, but are obliged to hold that medial י stands with medial ו for that very early lengthening of the inflective vowel by which the primary roots were made to assume a triliteral guise.

ע is an indeterminative in בער, to be separated from (represented in Heb., Arab., and Ethiopic) as compared with the universal root בר, to divide; also in בער, to cut off, consume (appearing in Heb., Aram., and Arabic) as related with the primitive root בר, to divide; so too evidently in צער, to be small (in Heb., Aram., and Arabic) as developed from צר, to press together, contract, also Proto-Semitic; and in several other cases, amounting to about one half of the whole number of roots in which ע appears as the middle radical. In nearly all the remainder with medial ע the first letter is a determinative: thus, it would seem, ע was not liked as the second letter of primitive biliterals, while, as we have seen, it was frequently employed as the first — an instructive fact in Semitic phonology and morphology.

These are the only letters we can regard as undoubted Proto-Semitic indeterminatives. Others (as נ, ר, ל, ת) were

106   RELATIONS OF THE ARYAN AND SEMITIC LANGUAGES.

used more or less freely in the different dialects during their separate history, especially in the formation of quadriliterals, which are all secondary roots.¹

Lastly, we have to take the final determinative letters in Proto-Semitic. These are much more numerous than either of the other two classes; the true place of the additional sounds in secondary roots being at the end, as in the Aryan family.

א represents a post-determinative very frequently. So in ברא, to hew out, fashion, create (in Heb., Aram., and Arabic), from בר, to cut, which is variously represented in all the dialects. So also in כלא, to shut out, to obstruct (Heb., Aram., and Arabic), as compared with כל, to shut, close, finish (found in noun or verb stems in all the dialects). It appears in many other examples that might be cited; and we are inclined to set it down as a principle that wherever א appears as the last letter of a root, it is of secondary origin, unless the first letter is a determinative. This might be inferred from the character of the sound itself, which only exists for the sake of its vowel; but it may be proved in nearly every case by actual comparison with kindred forms. The only instances in which this is not practicable are probably מלא, to fill; קנא, to be moved with passion; and צמא, to thirst; and here it is better to assume that the kindred roots are lost or their connection obscure, than to maintain that the א stands so exceptionally for an independent consonant.

ב is apparently a post-determinative in גרב, to be scabby, leprous (Heb., Aram., and Arabic in noun or verb stems), from the widespread root גר, to scrape; in חטב, to hew wood (Heb., Arab., and Ethiopic) from the common root חט, to cut; in צלב, to hang up = make incline (Aram., Arab., and

¹ If the Proto-Semitic root עתד to prepare, could be regarded as having a similar origin to that of جَعَلَ conj. VIII. in Arabic, an instance would be at hand of the use of ת servile as an indeterminative; but this we cannot regard as probable.

Ethiopic), as compared with צלא, to incline, also Proto-Semitic; and perhaps in a few other cases.

ג is a post-determinative in פלג, to divide (in various noun or verb stems in Aram., Heb., Arabic, and Ethiopic), from the root פל, to cleave, burst asunder, variously represented in all the dialects; and perhaps in גרג, to go, proceed by steps (Aram., Arabic, with a Heb. noun-stem), as compared with דרך, and the primary root דר, which seems to express lively motion in general. We cannot adduce any other probable instances from Proto-Semitic.

ד is a post-determinative in חמד, to be ardent (with related meaning in all the dialects[1]), as compared with חם, to be warm; also in פרד, to separate (in Heb., Aram., and Arabic), from פר, to rend asunder; and in several other cases.

ה is an post-determinative apparently in בלה, to be stupid, embarrassed, timid (cf. the Heb., Aram., and Arabic meanings), from בל, to be confounded, confused; probably in אלה, the root[2] of a Proto-Semitic name for God (Heb., Aram., and Arabic, which), as we prefer to think, is a denominative from the shorter אל, also proved to be Proto-Semitic by the Assyr. *il-u*; and, in general, wherever it occurs as the third radical, as it does but rarely in the primitive speech.

ו, or rather the vowel *u*, was used as a post-determinative in the primitive speech.[3] So apparently in גלו, to draw off, lay bare, reveal (in Heb., Aram., and Arabic; in Ethiopic, to draw on, cover), as compared with a root גל, evident in גלה, גלח, גלד, גלב, of kindred meanings, all Proto-Semitic. So too

---

[1] The Hebrew and Chaldee forms mean to desire ardently; the Arabic has one meaning, to be angry (or "warm"); another to deem worthy of praise, i.e. desirable; the Assyrian means to hasten, or pursue ardently.

[2] What the specific meaning of this root was, or whether it ever had more than a theoretical potential significance, is doubtful. The Arabic meaning, to adore, is probably secondary, = regard as God.

[3] It is not easy to say in all cases whether *u* or *i* was the original determinative vowel. It is only in Arabic and Ethiopic that the distinction between the two has been regularly preserved. Moreover, in these languages so many new roots were developed in later times with these as final sounds, that the question of priority is still further obscured. It is only where the two idioms agree in important roots, that we can infer surely as to the real state of the case.

108   RELATIONS OF THE ARYAN AND SEMITIC LANGUAGES.

in דלי, to let down, suspend, weigh (cf. the various related meanings in Assyr., Ethiop., Heb., Aram., and Arabic, which has also דלי), from the root דל, to hang loose, no less widely represented through the system; and in other cases that might be adduced.

ז is a post-determinative in ברז, to pierce. This root is found only in Heb. and Aram.; but it is proved to be Proto-Semitic by the word for iron, ברזל (פרזל), which is found in all the dialects, and is evidently developed from it, as we shall see later. The ultimate root is בר, to divide open, already frequently cited. פרד, to separate, branch out, is also Proto-Semitic, from the common root פר, related to בר. ז, however, is rarely used for this purpose, as we would naturally expect from the fact that it is a secondary sound arising from *s*: cf. in Hebrew פרו, פרס, פרץ; עלו, עלס, עלץ.

ח is a frequent post-determinative. So in ברח, to pass through, to pass out, escape (cf. the Heb., Arabic, and Ethiopic stems), as related with בר. So also in גלח, to make bare, smooth, bald (Heb., Aram., and Arabic), as compared with גלה, etc., cited above. It is found, besides, in a few other cases; but was employed far more frequently in each dialect after the dispersion of the family.

ט is perhaps a post-determinative in פלט, to break away, escape (cf. the related senses in Heb., Aram., and Arabic; the Assyr. בלט, to live = to be preserved, is the same root), from בל, to cleave or break open. Possibly, also, in חרט (Aram., Arabic, and Hebrew in noun or verb stems, and perhaps Assyrian) to cut into, grave, engrave, as compared with a root חר, represented in Arab. خَرَّ , to cut open, pierce, divide; in חרש, etc. The Heb. and Arab. שרט of like meaning, we may compare with a root שר, represented in the Heb. שור and שרר, to saw, and elsewhere. ט, however, was not a very common determinative.

י,[1] or rather the vowel *i*, was apparently the most common of all the post-determinatives. The following are a few of its examples: נכי, to smite, injure (Arab., Ethiop., Heb., and

---

[1] See the remarks just made on י as a post-determinative.

RELATIONS OF THE ARYAN AND SEMITIC LANGUAGES. 109

Aram.), from a common root גך, cognate with נג ; נקי, to be separate, pure (with interesting derived meanings in Arab., Aram., Heb., and Assyrian), as compared with נם, a widely represented primitive root, meaning to strike asunder; קני, to erect, to establish, acquire, possess (in noun or verb stems in all the dialects), from קן, to be erect.

ב is a probable post-determinative in דרך, to tread (with various associated meanings in Heb., Aram., and Arabo-Ethiopic), as compared with דרג and the primary די cited above. Also in פרך, to break in pieces, crush, oppress (cf. the noun and verb stems with related meanings in Syr., Arab., Heb., and Assyrian), from the familiar root פר, to rend asunder; and in a few other instances.

ל is a post-determinative in גרל, to twist together, make strong or great (cf. the various meanings in Aram., Heb., Arab., and Ethiopic), as related with the root גר, to bind, which appears in אגר and גיר, both Proto-Semitic. It is also found in גרל, to tear off, drag off, as related with גר, already cited (both of which are found in Heb., Aram., Arabic); and in a few other cases.

ם is a post-determinative in עצם, to be firm, strong, great (cf. the noun and verb stems in Arab., Heb., and Assyrian [1]), as related with עז, to be strong, as found in עצה, עיץ, etc. Also in ערם, to be naked, bare, as compared with עור and ערה, of a similar meaning, all of them being Proto-Semitic. A few other cases might be adduced.

ן as a Proto-Semitic post-determinative can hardly be proved. The only plausible instance we can adduce is גרן, the root of the Proto-Semitic word for threshing-floor (Heb., Arabic, and Ethiopic), which seems to be developed from a root גר, of manifold expressiveness, but having clearly the general sense of dragging along, rubbing, crushing, so that גרן may perhaps be = the place of threshing grain.[2] גבן, to

---

[1] The Assyr. *aṣmu* means material, analogous with Heb. עצם bone, in the Inscription of Khorsabad, line 164 (see Oppert's Commentaire philologique).

[2] There does not seem to be any verb-stem גרן clearly Proto-Semitic, which would give a suitable intermediary sense. The Arabic جَرَنَ, however, means

be curved or arched, if it is Proto-Semitic in that sense, might be connected with גב of kindred meaning; but it is difficult to comprehend all the divergent meanings of the former root under one general satisfactory notion. נ was used more freely for this purpose in each dialect after the family separation.

ס[1] is a post-determinative in פרס, to cleave asunder, break up (cf. the noun and verb stems in Heb., Aram., Arab., and Ethiopic) as related with the familiar root פר; and in a few other cases.

ע is a post-determinative in גרע, to hew off (Heb. and Arabic) from the root גר, variously represented in the sense of cutting; in זרע, to scatter, to sow (represented in Heb., Aram., Arab., Eth., and Assyrian), from the root זר, to spread, scatter, shown in זרי and several other kindred forms; and in many other cases. It is clearly a determinative in nearly every instance of its use as the last radical. Those few cases are of course excepted when the first letter is a determinative, as in רצע, to place; נטע, to set in or set out. It is probable that no ultimate triliteral ended in ע. שבע, to be full, satisfied, is probably no exception.[2] Those who hold to a common origin of סבע[3] and the Indo-European word for *seven* will have no hesitation in considering the ע as secondary in the former word.

פ is a post-determinative in גרף, to carry away, sweep away (in noun or verb-stems in Heb., Aram., Arab., Ethiop., and Assyrian), from the root גר, to drag along, already

to grind corn, thus furnishing a notion kindred to the one required. Its other meaning of smoothing, wiping clean, does not throw satisfactory light on the word for threshing-floor, though it is usually assumed as explaining it.

[1] The distinction between this and ש was, as we have seen, obscured in some of the dialects. The Hebrew ס appears to have preserved the sound best, though not in all cases. With it agrees in general, the Arabic س, the Ethiopic ሰ, the Aramaic ܣ and ס, and the Assyrian *s*, as it is conventionally represented; though the disagreements are frequent, except in Assyrian.

[2] See Gesenius' Thesaurus, p. 1319, for kindred forms.

[3] Not שבע. That the other is the Proto-Semitic form, a comparison of Assyrian *sibu* with the Arabic and Ethiopic shows plainly.

alluded to; in נגח (Heb., Aram., and Ethiopic), to smite, from the widespread root גנ, to strike; and in several other plain cases.

צ is a post-determinative in פרץ, to cleave or break open (Heb., Assyr., Arab., and Aramaic), from the common root פר, to divide; and in a few other instances equally clear.

ק is a post-determinative in זרק, to scatter, sprinkle (in noun or verb stems in Heb., Assyr., Aram., and Arabic), from the root זר already referred to; and in several other forms.

ר is a post-determinative in פשר, to open (with various associated meanings in Assyr., Heb., Aram., and Arabic), from the common root פש (פה) of kindred meaning; and in many other forms that might be cited.

ש is a post-determinative in פרש, to separate, scatter, disperse (Heb., פָּרַשׁ; Aram., ܦ݁ܪܰܫ and פְּרַשׁ; Arab., فَرَشَ; Assyr., פרש in Niphal, to flee away), from the familiar root פר. It appears besides in only a few other cases; but, like ס, was more commonly employed as a secondary formative in each dialect after the Semitic dispersion.

ת also is an infrequent post-determinative. It appears in צמת, to be silent and bring to silence (cf. the associated meanings in Heb., Syriac, Arabic, and Ethiopic), as related with the root צם, with the primary notion of binding, shutting up, which is extended in the different roots so as to express the divergent ideas of fasting, deafness, dumbness. It is found also in a few other cases, and in some instances of its occurrence the root is perhaps a denominative, formed from a feminine abstract.

We must now put together the results of this investigation into the structure of Semitic secondary roots, and try to classify those sounds used in forming them. First, as to predeterminatives, we found that א, ח, ו, ה (probably), י, מ, נ, ע, ש, and ת were thus used. Of these א represents only a prefixed vowel; for though it is a true consonant it is only used in the interest of the vowel sound that conditions it.

With regard to ו and י, it might seem doubtful whether they were originally prefixed as consonants, or as the corresponding vowels u and i. On the whole, we incline to the belief that they were at first vowels, and then in course of inflection hardened into semi-vowels. For this the following arguments may be offered: (1) the analogy of the post-determinatives ו and י; (2) the frequent interchange observed in every Semitic period of פו or פי with עי forms developed from the same primary root,— a phenomenon easy of explanation upon this theory, but more difficult upon the other; the עי stems being, as we have seen, merely vowel expansions of עע forms; (3) the fact that consonants are not normally liked as predeterminatives: מ, נ, ש, and ת are used because they are inflective formatives; the other consonants are breathings, and of them ה and ע are rare, and ח doubtful. In all probability we may set down א as representing a, ו and י as representing u and i respectively, when used as predeterminatives.

ה, ח, and ע, used as predeterminatives, probably arose in this way. ה is the surd breathing corresponding to the sonant א, and arose from it through the process of dialectic variation familiar in all languages. Its rarity as a radical prefix is a proof of its late employment for this purpose. From it ח arose by strengthening, and was employed still more rarely. ע is the deep guttural development of א; and as ח is rarer than ה, so ע is rarer than א as a predeterminative.

The true consonants used as radical prefixes, מ, נ, ש, ת, are among the rarest used as post-determinatives; while other consonants, some of which are very common at the end of roots, are not used at all as predeterminatives. The solution of this enigma can only be gained from the consideration that these are letters used frequently as prefixes in the formation of verb or noun stems. And it is remarkable that the frequency of their occurrence, respectively, varies according to the priority of their introduction as stem-formatives, as the phenomena of the Semitic idiom seem to indicate: נ is most commonly employed, then ש, ת coming next, and finally מ,

which seems to have been used for only a short time before the family dispersion.

We have, then, as Proto-Semitic predeterminatives the vowels *a, i, u* (which were displaced by the corresponding א, י, and ו, under the later consonantal system), the breathings ה, ח, and ע, and the consonants ז, ן, ש, and ת, originally inflective formatives, themselves relics of old independent stems or words. All of these, save the vowels *a, i, u*, were introduced in the consonantal period.

As indeterminatives we found the breathings א, ח, and ע to be used, and ה, which is rarest as a radical prefix, does not appear here at all, being too much like a true consonant. These all belong to the consonantal stage of Semitism, as also does the vowel expansion, already treated of, expressed currently by ו and י.[1]

As to post-determinatives, we found that all of the consonants, with the possible exception of נ, were so employed. א, ו, and י, however, represent vowels that were used as radical affixes before the establishment of the consonantal régime. As in Proto-Aryan, so in Proto-Semitic, the regular place for determinatives is the last part of the root. A study of the character of the prefixed and inserted radical letters, as compared with the post-determinatives, makes it probable that they would not have been used at all, except in the interest of a manifold development of roots; since the need of various expression, as ideas multiplied, could be met in no other way; the genius of Semitism, unlike that of Aryanism, being averse to the use of compound words.

There are a great many Proto-Semitic roots which, so far as can be seen, show no determinative letter; and there is, of course, every reason to suppose that many of these, as well as many of the Aryan roots, possessed three consonants from the beginning. Of quadriliterals there are no sure examples in verb-stems. In noun-stems there are a few whose triliteral origin is apparent.

---

[1] Of course there is no inconsistency in making א at the beginning represent a primary vowel, and in the middle a consonant; for a vowel must have been heard already in all vocal expressions beginning and ending with a consonant.

Two classes of cases yet remain to be considered. First, we have those triliterals in which the third radical is the same as the first. This form, which seems so inconsistent with the ordinary types of Semitic root-structure, is accounted for by an analysis of the roots in question, from which it appears that they are developed from shorter forms by the repetition of the first radical.[1] These also occur in noun-stems in Proto-Semitic, not in verb-stems, except, perhaps, in denominatives. They are common enough in the several dialects as developed later, where their origin can be clearly traced.

Another and very important class of secondary roots are those עי roots that end in א, as the Proto-Semitic בוא, to go in. With regard to such cases we claim, without hesitation, in accordance with the principles already established, that the root originally consisted of a consonant and a vowel. The root was raised later to the triliteral standard cnly graphically, and not in actual speech, just as the Hebrew לֹ, not, is sometimes written לֹא, though it was never anything in sound but *lô*. The fact is, that the Semitic roots, before the consonantal period, had as great variety of form as the Proto-Aryan. It is an error to maintain that all the Semitic roots are ultimately tri-consonantal; but it is also an error to hold either that all were developed from biliterals, or that in general the bi-consonantal form is their shortest or ultimate type.

Guided by the principles above set forth, we shall now attempt to draw up a scheme of the possible and actual root-forms in the two systems of speech.

I. A Proto-Aryan root may consist:

(1) Of a consonant and a vowel, as '*i*,[2] to go; *ḳi*, to lie down; *da*, to give.

---

[1] This throws light on the origin of a number of obscure words; for example, *báb* the Proto-Semitic word for gate is, as we conjecture, from the root בא, to go in, enter.

[2] The Greek ' is here used to represent the breathing, corresponding to א, which precedes every vowel-sound at the beginning of a word or syllable.

(2) Of a consonant, a vowel, and a consonant, as '*ad*, to eat; *pat*, to fall; *tar*, to go through.

(3) Of two consonants and a vowel, as *klu*, to shut; *pri*, to love; *pru* (*plu*), to swim.

(4) Of two consonants, a vowel, and a consonant, as *dram*, to run; *prak*, to ask; *prat*, to spread out.

(5) Of a consonant, a vowel, and two consonants, as *kart*, to cut; *bharg*, to shine; *mard*, to bruise.

(6) Of two consonants, a vowel, and two consonants, as *spargh*, to strive after; *smard*, to gnaw at.

A root in any of these classes but the first may be secondary. In class (5) probably all, in class (6) certainly all, are secondary.

II. A Proto-Semitic root (taking in both the preconsonantal and the consonantal period), might consist

(1) Of a consonant and a vowel,[1] as בוא < בא, to go, or go in (Heb., Ethiop., Arabic, and Assyrian); ראי < רא, to see (Heb., Arab., and Ethiopic).

(2) Of two consonants, as בר, to separate (represented in all the dialects); עז, to be strong (in all the dialects).

(3) Of two consonants with internal vowel expansion, as איל, to be strong, superior (Heb., Arab., and Assyr. in noun or verb stems); כון, to be set up, or established, exist (in all the dialects).

(4) Of a consonant, a consonant, and a vowel, as כלא, to shut up or out (in all the dialects); דלי, to let down, suspend (represented in all the dialects); נקי, to be separated, pure (represented in Arab., Aram., Heb., and Assyrian).

(5) Of a vowel, a consonant, and a consonant, as אבד, to be lost, perish (Heb., Aram., Ethiopic); יכל, to contain, be capable (Heb., Arab., and Assyrian); ישר, to be right, prosperous (in all the dialects).

(6) Of three consonants, as ברך, to kneel, bless (in all the dialects); קדש, to be pure, sacred (in all the dialects); שלט, to be strong, to rule (in all the dialects).

---

[1] In this classification a vowel is cited as an integral part of the root, only when it is original and determinate.

(7) Of four consonants. Noun-stems, as ברזל, iron (represented throughout the system), presuppose a true root; and פרשׂ, to spread out < פרשׂ, is certainly Proto-Semitic, being represented in Hebrew, Arabic, and Assyrian.

A root in any of these classes but the first and second may be secondary. In classes (4) and (5) probably all, and in class (7) certainly all, are secondary.

In the next Article we shall consider whether the morphological differences between the two systems of roots may be reconciled, and enter upon a comparison of the roots that may seem to invite such treatment.

CHAPTER V.

COMPARISON OF ROOTS.

HAVING in the last Chapter taken up the most important questions relating to the formation of the predicative roots, considered as primary and secondary, in the two systems of speech, and having presented a scheme of the typical forms under which these roots are expressed, it remains for us to determine how we may reconcile the seemingly discordant principles according to which they are formed. The main difficulty presented arises from this fact, that while in the Aryan system the vowel is a significant part of the root, in the Semitic, on the other hand, — at least in the inflectional period of that idiom, — the vowel is not essential to the expression of the radical idea. The difficulty is great, but perhaps not insurmountable. The following considerations are offered as tending to show that a reconciliation is possible:

(1) The Semitic principle of root structure bears evidence of a secondary and, so to speak, artificial origin. In the language as it is presented to us, the vowel is not co-ordinate with, but subordinate to, the consonant. Now, we do not claim that the vowel once held an equally important place with the consonant. If language is a growth, and not an institution, the two elements cannot have been originally co-ordinate, even in those systems of speech where we find them currently of equal value. The consonants, as the harder and more stable elements of speech, must have secured their independent recognition and employment before the vowels, in all early forms of human language. But it may be said that the Semitic is an exception to other systems in

this, that the vowels never secured complete autonomy for themselves. This is true; but it is not true that they always filled that subordinate function which we see assigned to them in the full-blown inflectional period. It has been shown already that vowels even formed a constituent part of distinct, independent roots; we have not only an internal vowel expansion, but also a development of secondary roots by the use of any one of the three original vowels *a, i, u*, each of which has maintained a distinct and clearly recognizable influence until the latest Semitic times. We have even found that some roots consisted of a consonant and a vowel; and if it cannot be clearly shown in each instance what that vowel was, it still remains true that, though it is there subordinate to the consonant, its subordination is of an essentially different kind from that which is seen in the function of vowels in the "strong" stems of the inflectional period; it is, in fact, due merely to that indefiniteness which we have shown to be necessary to the vowel in all primordial speech. It would, of course, be absurd to maintain that in the earliest Semitic the vowel was of equal importance with the consonant for the expression of radical ideas. But it would be just as absurd to hold that it counted for nothing. If there is anything which can be maintained with certainty as a necessary feature of primitive language in general, and of the constitution of its roots, it is this,—that in both the vowel played an independent part. On the other hand, the only sure induction from the phenomena of root development, as we have studied the subject, is, that the vowel was subordinate and fluctuating.[1]

(2) The Proto-Aryan roots also give evidence of a previous

[1] Here, as well as in related discussions, it makes no difference what theory is held as to the nature of "roots," whether we regard them as having once been actual words, or as being mere abstractions—forms theoretically assumed as the basis of actual words. Unless the distinction between primary and secondary roots, to whose elucidation the last chapter was devoted, is an utter delusion, we shall have, upon either theory, to go back of the current triliterals, if we wish to determine these ultimate forms to which the name of "root" is applied; and in the last analysis the indefiniteness as well as the originality of the vowel in such forms, will be equally apparent under either view.

stage in their history when the vowel did not possess the certain and stable character manifest in their current forms. At least, it is allowable to infer as much as this from the fact that so many forms are found expressing the same or kindred ideas which agree in their consonants and differ in their vowels. Thus we have *bhag*, to eat; *bhug*, to enjoy; *mand* and *mund*, to decorate; *mad*, to be excited; *mud*, to be gay, joyful; *skad* and *skid*, to split; *as* and *is*, to throw; *di* and *du* > *div*, to shine; *pa* and *pi*, to drink; *bhad* and *bhid*, to pierce, cleave; *si*, to bind, and *su*, to sew; *ska* and *sku*, to cover; and a multitude of other divergent associated forms.¹ These cannot very well be regarded as primary and secondary roots respectively, because there is no development of meaning and no addition or degeneration of form.²

At this point the two great systems of speech seem to meet We find Semitic roots in which the vowel is indeterminate, and yet an independent constituent; and we find Aryan roots with fixed consonants, but varying vowels. Both phenomena are just what would be expected in the necessary development of early language; and the subsequent divergence of the two idioms in root formation can also be explained. In both systems definiteness of expression was aimed at equally and necessarily. In the Aryan system this was secured by giving greater precision to the vowel elements in each utterance, till at last they were made co-ordinate with the consonants in every respect. In Semitic, on the other hand, the original vagueness of the vowel remained, and definiteness as well as variety of expression was sought through the multiplication of consonants, either with or without the use of determinative letters. Hence we are prepared to find that while the bulk of the current Aryan roots have two consonants, and are monosyllabic, the bulk of the Semitic have three, and were perhaps originally dissyllabic.

[1] Such forms may be collected and collated from Pott's Wurzel-Lexicon, or more readily from Fick's Vergl. Wörterbuch d. indogerm. Sprachen, Vol. i.

[2] This extensive group must be distinguished from that small class of forms with vowel variations which we cited in the last Chapter as consisting of secondary roots.

Hence also it happened that in Semitic the vowel elements had less precision and importance in each utterance, till at last they lost their independence entirely, and became subordinate to the consonants in every respect.[1]

From this it follows that whatever roots in the two idioms are to be adduced for comparison must be represented by their consonants alone. This, of course, need not be any bar to an association of such roots, if they are eligible in other respects. For even within the Aryan range alone a consonantal formula might often be chosen as comprehending the same idea under various vowel variations. Thus, in accordance with examples of roots just cited, *MD* might convey the general notion of highly wrought feeling, and S^o ($S +$ an indeterminate vowel) might stand for the idea of fastening together; just as in the Semitic sphere רם means to be high, and בא means to go.

We thus see how the Proto-Aryan and Proto-Semitic roots may be brought together, so far as the forms are concerned. It remains for us to determine what kinds of roots are to be compared as regards their signification.

(1) First, it is evident that we must exclude those roots which are clearly onomatopoetic. In many languages throughout the world we find the same or like forms occasionally used to express the same ideas, when the sound seems to be a sort of echo of the sense, as when words seem to be

---

[1] J. Grill, in an elaborate Essay in the Zeitschrift d. deutschen morgendl. Gesellschaft, Vol. xxvii. pp. 425–460, attempts to show that the roots of the two systems may be unified in structure by reducing them to a hypothetical stage of development in which the vowel *a* alone was heard in them all (p. 449). Under those circumstances he thinks the vowels would not count for anything as determining the specific expression of the root-idea, since they would be the same in all the forms. The validity of this conclusion depends upon the correctness of the assumption of such a form of speech, an "Alpha-Sprache" as he terms it. But there is no strong evidence of it. The preponderance of the vowel *a* in Aryan roots may be accounted for on the principle that it is the most common of sounds in general, not necessarily the only primary vowel. The reader is referred also to the criticisms upon the similar, but not so far-reaching, theory of Fick, made in our last Article. On the other hand, we have abundant evidence of the original vagueness and variations of the vowel-sounds in the roots of both systems.

simply imitative of the movements of the objects of nature, or of the utterances of men or lower animals. Some writers have made undue use of this fact, and applied it to the explanation of many cases in which onomatopeia has had no part. It offers an easy solution of innumerable difficulties, and can often be plausibly appealed to when no etymon is at hand to which a given form may be referred. Thus the comparer of obscure roots runs a double risk. On the one hand, he is liable to cite forms as being of kindred derivation whose likeness is due to their origin in the imitative tendencies of early speakers; and, on the other hand, he is in danger of being accused of citing cases which are all "more or less onomatopoetic," and therefore not necessarily of common origin. Now, while it is true that such a charge has often been made unjustly against etymologists, it is not to be denied that it has always been made with some justice against those who have attempted to compare Aryan and Semitic roots. It will be our aim to avoid occasion for such an accusation, except as it may come from those who see in onomatopoeia the universal solvent of etymological difficulties, and would therefore give no credit to any comparison whatever made within our present sphere.

(2) It is also evident that we ought to include only those forms which express common and elementary notions. This must be insisted upon rigorously; and the principle is adopted not only for our guidance, but also as our defence against the opponents of all attempts at comparison in this obscure region.

It is clear, in the first place, that if the two families were originally one they must have separated at a time when only the most rudimentary arts of life were practised, and the most primitive conceptions of the world without and within the mind were attained. Hence a combination of forms conveying conceptions peculiar to a more advanced state of thought must be regarded with suspicion. Coincidences between forms expressing such notions are, indeed, not common; but they have been used too freely by comparers, and discredit has thus been cast upon such investigations in general.

It is manifest, in the second place, that if a large number of notions clearly elementary are found to be expressed in the two idioms by like sounds, in whose production onomatopoeia has had no share, the evidence in favor of previous unity is very strong. We have not only the fact of a coincidence of such words as we should expect to find agreeing, but also the consideration that the occurrence of such coincidences ought, if we judge from the analogy of languages in general, to argue the existence at one time of many more similar phenomena which are now lost to view. For if we regard any great family of tongues,— the Aryan, for example,— it is surprising, as well as instructive for our present purpose, to note how many of the most elementary notions are expressed differently in the different dialects, and how many expressions once common to the whole family have been dropped in one or several of them in the course of ages. We must not, and ought not, from the very nature of the question, to look for many agreements; and if, after all, the number is found to be considerable, the evidence in favor of an original unity, which rises with cumulative force with every additional case, becomes well-nigh irresistible.

These, then, are the conditions under which forms may be cited for comparison. If it is urged that it is not always easy to determine what notions are primary or elementary, and what are secondary, the answer is that we are not left to *a priori* judgments alone in the matter; for the science of etymology has pushed its researches into various languages so far and so successfully that we can appeal to the analogy of similar developments outside our proper sphere; and this is the surest resource for those who seek to have light thrown upon the workings of the human mind as they are revealed in language.

Words in common relating to Fire.

If the Aryans and Semites came from a common stock we should expect to find some trace of their early civilization in their common possession of one or more words for burning.

Fire was one of the earliest discoveries of mankind, and plays an important part in the legendary and mythical systems of most primitive communities. The fact is that we find no less than four words belonging to both systems, comprising most of the Proto-Aryan terms relating to that subject, and a large part of the Proto-Semitic.

1. Proto-Aryan ḳav (ḳu); Proto-Semitic כב, to burn.

The Proto-Aryan character of the root is proved by the following forms: Gr. καίω for καϜ-ίω, to burn; Skr. çona (for primary kau-na) flaming red, and as a noun, fire (see the Petersburg Dict., and cf. Curtius, 5.ed., p. 145; Fick i. p. 61). That it was developed from an earlier ḳu appears further from the occurrence of secondary roots, meaning to shine, most of which are found only in Sanskrit; one, however, ḳvid (whence Eng. *white*) being Proto-Aryan. — For the Proto-Semitic root we may compare Heb. כָּיָה, Assyr. kav-u,[1] Arab. كَوَى, Syr. ܟܘܐ, to burn. The root כב here inherent was probably developed from an earlier כו like the Proto-Aryan, though this is not essential to the validity of the comparison.

2. Proto-Aryan kad (kand); Proto-Semitic קד, to burn.

This is one of the most wide-spread of Porto-Aryan roots. In Sanskrit it appears in some of its senses with a prothetic *s* (cf. *tan* and *stan*, to sound), in the sense of glowing, for according to the Petersburg Dict. the root *cand*, to shine, is from *çcand*. But *kand-u*, a fire-pan, shows no trace of it. Nor do any of the hometymous forms outside the Sanskrit, unless the Gr. ξανθ-ός, yellow, is connected with the root. Gr. κάνδ-αρος, a coal, Lat. *cand-ere*, *cand-idus*, *in-cend-o*, Anglo-Saxon *hât* = Eng. *hot*, are a few out of the many examples that might be adduced. Remotely related seems to be the Skr. çudh (for kudh), to purify, which is probably a by-form of *kadh* found in Gr. καθ-αρός, pure and Lat. *cas-tus* for *cad-tus*. The assumption that the form with *s* is primary (Fick,

---

[1] In these special comparisons when the Assyrian roots are represented by the Kal infinitive, *u* must be understood to be the formative suffix. Sometimes they will be indicated by the consonants alone.

i. p. 241; Curtius, p. 522) is due to an over-deference to the Sanskrit. The primary form is *kad*; the principle of nasalization resulting in *kand*, and the use of a prothetic *s* in cases similar to the present, were discussed in our last Article. The Proto-Semitic קר is illustrated by the Heb. קָרַ, Arab. وَقَدَ, Syr. ܡܨܡ, to burn, in which ר is a predeterminative. Also by the Heb. קרח, to kindle fire, Arab. قَدَحَ, and Syr. ܣܡܒ, of similar meaning, in which the ח is a post-determinative.

3. Proto-Aryan *kar* (*kal*), to heat, to cook; Proto-Semitic קל, to roast, to fry.

kar (*kal*) is represented by Skr. *çrâ*, to boil, cook, from *çar* (= *kar*) as *mnâ* from *man*; Lat. *cal-eo, cal-or, cre-mare*, and several other Aryan forms — קל appears with a post-determinative vowel in Heb. קָלָה, Arab. قَلَى and قَلَا, and Ethiop. ቀለወ, to fry, Chald. קְלָא, to roast, to burn, Assyr. *kal-u*, to burn. This is perhaps the most striking combination of all the group; for we see here that a term used by both families in the sense of burning was also specialized in both so as to apply to the preparation of food by fire.

4. Proto-Aryan *us*, to burn; Proto-Semitic אש, fire (probably = the burning thing).

Skr. *ush*, to burn, scorch; Gr. αὔ-ω for αὔσ-ω, to kindle, εὔ-ω for εὔσ-ω, to singe; Lat. *ur-o* for *us-o*, to burn; Old Norse *us-li*, fire; A. S. *ys-el*, O. H. Germ. *us-el*, ashes.—Cf. Heb. אֵשׁ, Chald. אֶשָּׁא, Syr. ܐܫܬܐ, Eth. እሳት, Assyr. *'is-u*, fire. There is also an Aryan by-form *vas*, to enlighten, which is commonly thought to be the earlier root. Whether the Semitic words have arisen from וש, through the dropping of the original *v* or *w*,[1] or whether they themselves represent the earlier form, must remain undecided. This combination is highly probable, though not so certain as the other three.

In accounting for the common possession of these similar

---

[1] According to the usage which became universal in Assyrian. — Fick (ii. p. 27) combines the Teutonic word for ashes, *as-gan*, with the Lat. *ar-eo* for *as-eo* and *ard-eo* for *asd-eo*, pointing to a root *as*, to be hot.

forms, it is apparent that onomatopoeia must be excluded, as well as the theory of a chance coincidence. The only refuge left to doubters is the assumption that one language borrowed the sounds from the other. But why there should have been any borrowing at all of such primitive essential matters, or why it should have been done on so large a scale, is not easy to imagine.

WORDS FOR SHINING.

5. Proto-Aryan *bhar* (*bhal*); Proto-Semitic בהר (בר), to shine.

The Proto-Aryan form points, according to what was said on comparative phonology, to an earlier *bar*. It is represented in Skr. *bhâl-a*, star and brightness, *bhâl-u*, sun (also in *bhalla*, etc. a bear, from its sleekness?) Gr. φαλ-ηρός, shining; φαλ-ιός, white; Lith. *bál-ti*, to be white, with other Slavonic words cited by Fick (i. p. 152). Curtius (p. 297) suggests that there may have been no root *bhal* (*bhar*) at all, but that *la* may have a nominal suffix attached to the common root *bha*, to shine. The Slavonic forms seem to exclude this, and also the circumstance that there are two roots *bharg* and *bhark*, of similar meaning, which can only be regarded as secondaries from an intermediate *bhar*. — In Semitic we cite the Heb. בהר as in בָּהִיר, brilliant; Assyr. *buhar-u* and *bûr-u*, splendor; Arab. بَهَرَ, to shine; Syr. ܨܡܚ, in Shaphel, to glorify, like conj. III. of بَهَرَ. In these ה is an indeterminative; cf. Eth. ᐱᕈሀ, to shine forth, and Arab. بُرْهَان, a clear proof.

6. The Proto-Aryan *bha*, to shine, above referred to, we might plausibly compare with a hypothetical Proto-Semitic בה shown in בחק, בהג, בהה, to be white, glistening, variously represented in Heb., Syr., and Arabic. This would require us to assume that a strong breathing was developed independently in Semitic. The combination is very instructive in the light of others of the same group that are more harmonious.

7. Proto-Aryan *bhark̞* (*bhrak̞*), to shine, gleam; Proto-Semitic ברק, to shine, lighten.

Cf. Skr. *bhrâç* (abundantly attested by the grammarians, though not proved in the classical writings; see the Petersburg Dict.), for *bhrâk̞*, to shine; Gr. φορκ-ός, white, shining (Hesychius); Goth. *bairh-to*, bright, cf. Eng. *bright*, with other Teutonic as well as Slavonic forms, cited by Fick, i. p. 152.— For Semitic correspondences, cf. Arab. بَرَقَ, Syr. ܨܡܥ, Eth. ብረቀ, to shine, and to lighten; Heb. בָּרַק, to lighten, and בָּרָק, lightning, Assyr. ברק, whence *birk̞-u* lightning.[1]

8. Proto-Aryan *bharg*, to shine; Proto-Semitic בלג, to shine.

Cf. Skr. *bhrâj*, Zend *barâz*, to shine; Gr. φλέγ-ω, to shine, burn; Lat. *flag-ro*, to burn; A. S. *blíc-an*, to shine (cf. Eng. *bleach*, and Germ. *bleich*).— In Semitic we have the Heb. בָּלַג (in Hiph.), to be bright, cheerful, Arab. بَلَجَ, to shine forth, be clear. This Proto-Semitic root has no associations with any forms with medial ב, and in consideration of the essential character of the *l* sound, we may without presumption assign it to the root בר exemplified in the foregoing cases.

Accepting number 6. as a highly probable combination, we have in Proto-Aryan *bhâ* > *bhar* > *bhark* and *bharg*. The last three forms are the principal ones developed from *bhâ*, and with them we find in Semitic exact correspondences in form and sense, which seem to preclude the possibility of merely accidental resemblance.

---

[1] See this with other forms in Assyrian established by Lenormant, Étude sur quelques parties des syllabaires cunéiformes, p. 231. Most of the Semitic words mean both to be bright and to lighten, and though the latter predominates, the former is the primary sense. The resemblance of ברק to many words meaning to cleave, split, might suggest that the word for lightning arose from this notion, and that the sense of shining was secondary. But the natural order of the ideas, as well as the analogy of other languages, shows that the name for lightning was drawn from the idea of its brightness. So with our word itself, with the German *Blitz*, the French *éclair*, the Latin *fulgur*, and even *fulmen*.

RELATIONS OF THE ARYAN AND SEMITIC LANGUAGES. 127

9. Proto-Aryan *bhas;* Proto-Semitic בץ, בש, to shine.
The Proto-Aryan character of *bhas* is pretty safely established by Fick, i. p. 153. Cf. Skr. *bhâs*, to shine, *bhâs*, *bhâs-u*, splendor; Zend *banh*, light (*nh* for a primary *s*; see Schleicher, Compendium d. vergl. Gramm. 4. ed. p. 190), with Slavo-Teutonic *bas-a*, bare, manifest = Eng. *bare*.— In Semitic we have the form בץ clearly presented in Arab. وَبَصَ, to shine, probably appearing also in Heb. pr. noun בֶּצֶץ; cf. بَصَّ, to be white, shining, بَاضَ and بَاصَ, Heb. בוץ > בֵּיצָה *egg*,[1] with hometymous noun-stems in Aramaic and Arabic. The root בש seems to convey the same idea, for we find וָבֵשׁ along with וָבֵץ with a like meaning; cf. بَشْبَشَ and بَشَرَ, to be joyful. The last named root suggests the Proto-Semitic name for flesh, which we may represent by Heb. בָּשָׂר. It was probably so called from its bright color. Perhaps בשל, a Semitic word for cooking, came from the same source, as Lat. *frig-o*, Gr. φρύγ-ω, to roast, are connected with the root *bharg* (No. 8).

10. Proto-Aryan *ark* (*rak*); Proto-Semitic רק, to shine.
The root *ark* is proved from the Skr. *arc*, to shine forth, *arc-is*, splendor, and especially *ark-as*, the sun, as compared with Gr. ἠ-λέκ-τωρ, the sun, or sun-god. See Curtius, 5 ed., p. 137. Fick, i. p. 22, cites a number of Keltic words pointing to the root *lak* < *rak* as the Gr. ἠλέκ-τωρ as well as ἤλεκ-τρον, amber, point to a root *alk* < *ark*. With *rak* we may connect as a by-form the common Proto-Aryan root *ruk* (*luk*), to shine, and with *ark* the root *arg* of the same meaning, whence Skr., Zend, Gr., Lat., and Oscan words for silver. *ark* : *arg* = *rak* : *rag*, to color, a wide-spread Proto-Aryan root. The root *râg*, to shine forth, is a further devel-

---

[1] Mühlau and Volck in their edition (the eighth) of Gesenius Handwörterbuch (Leipzig, 1878), make the notion of whiteness, shining, to be secondary, and derived from the words for egg in the different dialects. But our citation of verb-stems shows this to be impossible. Cf. the derivation of *albumen*.

opment, whence the Skr. *rág*, to shine, and the Proto-Aryan word for king.—The existence of the corresponding Semitic root רק is not so evident at first, but is easily established. It appears most usually represented with a predeterminative י as in ירק, whose sense of shining is attested by its derivatives in all the dialects. The predominant meaning is to be yellow, whence a name for gold: Eth. ወርቅ, Arab. وَرِق, coined money; cf. Heb. יְרַקְרַק, as applied to gold, Ps. lxviii. 14, Assyr. *raḳraḳḳu*, yellow,[1] also *arḳu* and *araḳu*, yellow, green; Heb. יָרָק, green; יֶרֶק, Syr. ܝܽܘܪܳܩܳܐ, green herbs. Cf. also Heb. יֵרָקוֹן, paleness, yellowness, which like Arab. يَرَقَان, also أَرَق, denotes a disease in men, and a blight in grain, producing a yellow complexion. These several meanings can only be explained from the comprehensive sense of shining inherent in the root.[2] But we have the root in a simpler form, which puts this meaning beyond doubt. From some of the Assyrian and Arabic forms above cited, it appears that the י is not primary. Now we cite further, Arab. رَأَى, med. Waw, to be bright, clear (used of wine and the eyes); رَاقَ, med. Ye, to shine brightly (used of the *mirage*); رَقْرَقَ, to shimmer. Still further, the Arab. أَلَقَ, to shine, and أَلَق, splendor, show that here as well as in Greek and Keltic the primary *r* was sometimes replaced by an *l*; and a comparison of all the Semitic words shows clearly that the primary form was רק, which is thus assimilated perfectly to the Proto-Aryan *ark* or *ruk*.

---

[1] See Friedr. Delitzsch, Assyr. Studien. i. p. 105.

[2] The most instructive analogy that we know of is the Proto-Aryan root *ghar*. Meaning primarily to shine or glow, a large number of its derivatives show the signification of being yellow or golden, and green. So the Skr. *harita*, green and yellow, *hiraṇa*, gold, Gr. χρυσός, gold, for χρυτ-ιός, and Goth. *gulth*, Eng. *gold*. Derivatives are even found in Zend and Slavonic (see Fick, i. p. 81), having the sense of green shoots of plants, as with ירק.

Words for Cutting and Separating.

11. Proto-Aryan *bhar*; Proto-Semitic בר, to cut, to pierce.
The value of these roots in the present discussion is their agreement not simply in the general sense, but in two allied meanings. For *bhar*, cf. Zend *bar*, to cut, to bore; Gr. φάρ-ος, a plough, φάρ-αγξ, a cleft, ravine, φάρ-υγξ, opening, gullet; Lat. *for-are*, Eng. *bore*.—בר is illustrated by the Heb. בָּרָה, to cut; Arab. بَرَى ، بَرَا , to hew, hew out; Assyr. ברה,[1] to cut into, grave; also by ברא, to cut out, form, create, represented in most of the dialects. It shows also in forms with consonantal postdeterminatives, as ברז, to pierce, the root of the Proto-Semitic בַרְזֶל, iron. ברח, to pass through, seems to have had the same origin, if we may judge from the Assyr. *buruḫi*, spear.[2] Arab. بَرَتَ, to cut, appears in بَرْتٌ, cutting, بَرْتٌ, an axe; cf. Eth· ብርት, bronze, from the same root, as בַּרְזֶל, iron, < ברז. Naturally the simple form בר has mainly the general primary sense of separating, but in Ethiopic we have በረረ, meaning to pass through, perforate. The idea of boring, however, is most distinctively conveyed by the form with indeterminative א, באר (as in the Arab. بَأَرَ, to pierce), whence the word for a well in Heb., Syr., Arab., and Assyrian. Again the Arab. بَارَ, to explore, investigate = Heb. ביר (Eccl. ix. 1), points clearly to the same origin with a figurative application. With a stronger indeterminative, בער means to cut off, consume (with various associated senses in most of the dialects); and with a predeterminative, חבר means to divide up, in Hebrew and Arabic.

12. Proto-Aryan *bhad* (*bhid*); Proto-Semitic בד, to divide, split open.
Cf. Skr. *bhid*, to split; Lat. *find-o, fid-i*; Goth. *beit-an*, A. S. *bit-an* = Eng. *bite*. The Lat. *fod-io*, to dig; cf. Gr.

---

[1] A very probable root; see Friedr. Delitzsch, Assyrische Studien, i. p. 9.
[2] See Schrader, Keilinschriften u. d. Alte Testament, p. 106.

βόθ-ρος, a pit, seems to point to an old by-form *bhad*.—The root בר has a considerable development. In Heb. בָּד means to divide, and keep apart = Arab. بَلَّ, the same root having derivatives in Aramaic also; with ל as a post-determinative, בָּדַל means to divide, and with p the primary meaning of splitting comes out in בָּרַק, to cleave. With ע as an indeterminative, we have בצר, to separate from, represented by noun or verb stems, in Heb., Arab., and Ethiopic. The physical notion of cutting asunder is better preserved in the kindred root בת, which has a wide representation throughout the Semitic system.

13. Proto-Aryan *pat*; Proto-Semitic פת, פש, to separate, open.

These roots apparently stand remotely connected with No. 12. We find *pat* represented by the common consent of leading etymologists (see Fick, i. p. 135; Curtius, 5 ed., p. 211; Pott, W. Wb., iv. p. 154), in the Gr. πίτ-νημι, πετ-άννυμι, to spread out, open out, and πέτ-αλος, spread out; Lat. *pat-eo*, to open, and *pat-ulus* = πέτ-αλος; A. S. *fath-m*, the out-spread arms = Eng. *fathom*. We should also add, with Fick, the Zend *path-ana*, wide.—The Semitic פת has the fundamental notion of separating. So the Heb. פת, with the corresponding Arabic and Ethiopic, means to break off; hence various noun-stems in these dialects, meaning a fragment or morsel, or, as we say, a *bit* (see No. 12). But the simplest modifications of the root have precisely the sense that predominates in Proto-Aryan. Thus the Heb. פתה, as illustrated by the Arab. فَاتَ and its own derivative פת, means to spread out, while פתח,[1] in Heb., Aram., and Assyr., signifies to spread out and open. In Heb. and Syr., Arab. and Eth., פתח means also to open, while in Heb. פָּטַר means to open; and פָּתַר, to interpret, has developed its meaning obviously from the same primary notion. Cf. פשר, to cleave, open, in Heb., Assyr., and Arab., from a kindred root, פש.

[1] The name יֶפֶת, Japhet, of the ancestor of the Aryan race, from פתח, is an historical, if not a linguistic, connecting link between the two families.

RELATIONS OF THE ARYAN AND SEMITIC LANGUAGES. 131

14. Proto-Aryan *park̯*; Proto-Semitic פרק and פרך, to cleave.

The root *park̯* does not appear in any Aryan verb-stem, but we assume it to be represented in the Skr. *paraç-u* (cf. *parç-u*, *paraç-vadha*, *parç-vadha*), an axe or hatchet, and the corresponding Gr. πέλεκ-υς > πελεκ-ίζω, to hew off. Curtius, (5 ed., p. 164), refers these forms to a root πλακ, to beat, from which πλαγ in πλήσσω and Lat. *plang-o* arise through softening. That this is wrong seems to us clear, because (1) the Sanskrit forms show clearly that the original root was not *prak* but *park̯*, and (2) all the Greek and Sanskrit words contain only the idea of hewing or cleaving, and not of beating (wood-cutting is the most common notion in both languages). The root is *park̯*, and it can be explained only in the sense of cutting or cleaving.— In Semitic the root פרק is much more widely extended. In Heb., and Aram., and Ethiopic, its general secondary sense is that of separating and loosening; but the primary physical notion of cleaving is apparent also in Heb. as well as in Arabic. The kindred פרך has the prevailing signification of breaking up, but in Assyrian it takes the place also of פרק, meaning to separate, as well as to break in pieces. In all these dialects the root is represented largely in noun, as well as in verb stems. A very remarkable coincidence with the Proto-Aryan word is found in the Syr. ܦܠܩܐ, Assyr. *pilakki*, hatchet.[1] The root פלק, found besides in Arabic, and perhaps in Ethiopic, in the same sense, stands for the primary פרק, as the root פל, having the same general meaning of cleaving, is from פר, both of these latter being widely represented throughout the Semitic family with various determinatives. It is not claimed here that the Syrian and Assyrian word for hatchet is the same as the Proto-Aryan above cited. But both are apparently from the same root, and they show that this root in Aryo-Semitic expressed the special sense of cleaving or hewing wood.

15. Proto-Aryan *kar*; Proto-Semitic קר, כר, to cut, divide.

[1] See Friedr. Delitzsch, Assyr. Studien, i. p. 132 f.

The root *kar* is discussed fully by Pott, Wurzelwörterbuch, ii. p. 149 ff. It is also dealt with by Fick, i. p. 238 f., and Curtius, p. 147 f. The form *skar* appears in some of the dialects, but *kar* predominates, and is rightly taken by Pott as the proper root. It is found not only in Skr. *kar* (*kṛ-ṇámi* and *kṛ-ṇomi*,), to wound, but also in *kar, kar-omi*, to make, (cf. Eng. *shape* and *shave*, Heb. ברא, to hew out, and create). It also appears in Zend *kar*, to cut, and *kar-eta*, a knife, in Gr. κείρω for κερ-ίω, to shear, as well as in several noun-stems. The Latin has *cer-no*, to divide, as well as *cur-tus*, short (= cut off), and in the secondary sense, *cre-o, caerimonia*. The Goth. *hair-us*, sword, and the A. S. *hri-dder*, sieve, Eng. *riddle*, also belong here, the occurrence of which in the Teutonic family shows that the *skar* represented in Eng. *shear, scar*, and *score*, is a secondary root.—The existence of the כר in this sense is proved from the Heb. כָּרָה, Arab. كَرَ, Eth. ከረየ, Chald. כְּרָא, to pierce, to dig. The root בּוּר had probably the same sense in Heb., and Arab. קר again appears with a like meaning in Heb. קוּר, to dig out; Arab. قَالَ, to cut out; also with various determinatives in special modifications of the general notion of cutting.

16. Proto-Aryan *kart*; Proto-Semitic קרט, ברת, to cut off.

The root *kar* (No. 15), is developed into *kart* by the determinative *t* (cf. Pott, Wurzelwörterbuch, iv. p. 115). It is found in Skr. *kart, kṛint-ati*, to cut, split; Lith. *kert-ù*, to hew, *kirt-ikas*, a hewer, and various other Slavonic words cited by Fick (i. p. 46). The Latin *culter*, knife, is adjudged to belong here by Pott (ii. p. 152) being for *cult-ter;* cf. Skr. *kart-trî*, shears, and *kart-ari*, hunting-knife.—The occurrence of the root in Proto-Semitic seems clear. The Heb. ברת, to cut off, has no direct representative in the other dialects; but كَرْتَع, short, كَرْتوم, a rock, كَرْتِيم, an axe, show that it once existed in Arabic; and قَرَط, to cut up, with the Amharic ቀረጠ, of the same meaning, are matched by the Syr. ܩܪܛ.

All of these cannot have been developed independently of one another, and have therefore come from one primary form answering to the Proto-Aryan *kart*.

17. Proto-Aryan *karp* (*kalp*) ; Proto-Semitic קרם (קלם), to cut off.

The root *karp* (of which *skarp* is a further development), has a manifold representation in the Aryan tongues. It is an expansion of the root *kar* (No. 15, cf. Pott, Wurzelwörterbuch ii. p. 155, Etym. Forschungen, ii. p. 274 f.), with the determinative *p*, as *kart* (No. 16) is the same root developed by *t*. It is found in Skr. *kalp*, to cut up (only quotable in Prâkrit, but proved to be primitive from the derivatives), *krp-âna*, a sword, *kalp-aka*, a barber, *krp-âni*, shears ; cf. Lith. *kerp-u*, *kirp-ti*, to cut off, clip, with other Slavonic words cited by Pott. Probably Latin *carp-o*, to pluck off, belongs here ; cf. *dis-cerpo*. And, as Pott suggests, the Teutonic word *half* (A. S. *healf*, O. H. German *halb*), probably meant originally an equal division, and is thus naturally to be connected with this root.—On the Semitic side of the equation we find Arab. قَلَفَ, Eth. ቀለፈ, also Syr. ܩܠܦ, Chald. קְלַף, to tear off, peck off ; cf. Arab. قَرَفَ, and Eth. ቀረፈ, of the same meaning. We might be tempted to bring in here כלם, which is the root of the Heb. כֵּילַפּוֹת, axes of a certain sort (Ps. lxxiv. 6), a word to which there are similar terms in Syriac and Chaldee, but as these forms may be onomatopoetic they must be excluded.

18. Proto-Aryan *kars*; Proto-Semitic קרץ, קרש, to cleave, tear asunder, drag off.

The root *kars* has mostly the sense of dragging away, a meaning which it is not difficult to connect with that of separating. So the Skr. *karsh*, *karsh-ati*, means to drag, but also to tear,[1] and *karsh*, *krsh-ati*, means to plough, that is, to tear or divide the land, to make, not to draw,[2] furrows. Hence,

---

[1] Cf. the German *zerren*, to drag, also to tear, the latter being the primary sense = Engl. *tear*. How this can indicate violent motion is shown by our colloquialism "he tore along."

[2] Ploughing, in this expression, is usually explained (see Petersburg and

the derivative *karsh-û* means a furrow, but also an incision in general. The sense of dragging is therefore secondary, though as the root evidently implied originally a violent separating, that meaning arose very early, and is exhibited in those European forms which seem to represent the Skr. *karsh*. The root probably appears in the Gr. κορ-έω, to sweep out or away, if this is for κορσ-έω, as the Lat. *verr-o* for *vers-o*, and this for *cvers-o* would seem to imply. This combination which seems bold, has the high authority of Corssen in its favor. It certainly is the best that has yet been attempted. The root may be regarded almost certainly as Proto-Aryan, especially as all its meanings in Sanskrit appear also in Zend with corresponding forms. Perhaps a trace of the original sense of cutting off remains in Gr. κορσ-όω, to cut the hair, and κόρσ-η, the temples (as being shorn; but cf. Pott, W.Wb. ii. p. 157).—Of the corresponding Semitic roots the radical idea is also that of violent separation. So in Heb. קרץ, to cut off, also tear away (Job xxxiii. 6). Cf. Arab. قَرَصَ, to cut off, break off; قُرْصٌ, a morsel = Chald. קְרַץ, Syr. ܩܪܰܨ; Eth. ፀፈጸ, to cut into, engrave; also Arab. قَرَضَ, to cut off, gnaw off; Eth. ፀፈፀ, to cut off, tear off, shear. In these roots the fundamental notion of the Proto-Aryan *kars* is fully represented. Its secondary sense of dragging comes out in the Arab. قَرَشَ, which, like the Heb. קָרַשׁ, means first to cut off, but also, and more characteristically, to draw to one's self, to acquire. We also venture to add here the root חרץ, to cut, cleave, open, represented in Heb., Arab., Aram., and Assyrian; and especially the root חרשׁ, which, having the general sense of cutting open, furnished also the Proto-Semitic word for ploughing, Heb. חרשׁ (cf. Arab. حَرَثَ, Syr. ܚܪܰܬ), Eth. ሐረሰ. Cf. Assyr. *hirs-u*, a ploughed furrow (Lenormant, Benfey's Dictionaries) as the drawing of furrows. But the notion of drawing does not naturally yield that of ploughing, which is expressed by words for cutting or separating in all the cases that we can recall in both Aryan and Semitic.

op. cit. pp. 155, 202). This brings the Semitic word completely into accord with the Aryan *kars* in all its meanings. In this instance we do not hesitate to regard the roots as by-forms, the ק being weakened into ח, a change of frequent occurrence. That these letters are here of the same origin is as good as proved by the following correspondences, running through all the forms we have cited: קרט = (חרת) חרט; קרץ = קרש, חרץ = חרש, (קלף) קרף = חרף; (קרח). The agreement in meaning between each of these pairs is complete.

19. Proto-Aryan *sak*; Proto-Semitic שׂק, שׂך, to cut.

The root *sak* appears in Lat. *sec-o*, to cut; *sec-uris*, an axe; in *sec-tor* and *seg-mentum* as well as in *sic-a*, a dagger, and *sec-ula*, a sickle; also in various Slavonic words cited by Fick (i. p. 790), and Pott (iii. p. 322). It is also the basis of many Teutonic words; among them, that from which the Eng. *see*[1] (A. S. *se-on*, for *seh-wan*) is formed. With this the Teutonic word for a *saw* (*saga*) is allied, but not hometymous. The root is not found in Sanskrit or Zend, but, as Fick says, it is the basis of the Proto-Aryan *ska* (> Skr. *kshan*, to wound, and Gr. κτεί-ν-ω, κτά-μεναι), and there is no doubt that it belonged to the primitive stock.—שׂך is represented by Heb. שֵׂךְ, thorns, and שִׂכָּה, a sharp weapon; cf. Arab. شَوْكَة, Eth. ሦክ, a thorn, شَاكِي, armed with sharp weapons; also شَكّ, to be in doubt (i.e. divided in mind), and شَكَّة, weapons. שׂק appears in Arab. شَقّ, to cleave, with many derivatives; cf. Syr. ܫܩܰܩ, to cleave, > ܫܶܩܳܩܳܐ, a fissure. Both שׂך and שׂק are also found as secondary roots with various determinatives.

20. Proto-Aryan *tak*; Proto-Semitic תך, to cut, divide.

The root *tak* has the sense of forming, producing (as in Gr. τίκ-τω, ἔ-τεκ-ον, to beget), along with other meanings easily connected with it (see Fick, i. p. 86; Pott, W. Wb., ii. 2. 401 ff.;

---

[1] For the development of meaning, cf. the Lat. *cerno* and Germ. *unterscheiden*, meaning first to separate; Heb ריח, and Arab. بَصَر, to see, primarily to cut.

Curtius, p. 219 f.). What the primary meaning was, may perhaps be inferred from the secondary *taks*, which in Sanskrit means to hew out, to prepare, to make, and gives the noun *taksh-an*, a carpenter, a wood-cutter, *taksh-aṇa*, an axe. The Zend also has *tash*, to cut (from *taks* = O. Pers. *takhsh*, to build), and *tash-a*, an axe. From the same root comes Gr. τέκτ-ων, a carpenter, for τέκσ-ων. Finding that *taks* has properly the sense of cutting, we may turn back to the root *tak*, and we find that the Lat. *tig-num*, a beam, a log, is not from *taks*, but from *tak*, and it means evidently what is shaped by hewing. Further, the analogy of similar expressions elsewhere is in favor of this hypothesis. So especially with ברא (No. 11), which means (1) to hew out, (2) to form, or create, (3) to beget (cf. the Aram., word for son, בַּר, found also in Assyrian).—The meaning of the Semitic דך, appears from Arab. جَكَّ, to cut, to cut off, in Heb., figuratively, to injure. Cf. Syr. ܟܐ, to cut into, to injure. Again, the Heb. תוך, means to divide, as appears from תָּוֶךְ, the middle, i.e. the dividing point.

We have thus taken up nine pairs of roots belonging to the two families, having in common the primary sense of cutting or dividing, agreeing moreover perfectly in their primary forms. The most remarkable set of correspondences must be admitted to be found in the forms *kar*, *kart*, *karp*, *kars*, with their Semitic equivalents. The root *kar*, to cut, has no other secondary forms than these; they are all matched in Proto-Semitic. It is to be noted that some of these pairs of roots agree not only in their general sense, but also most strikingly in their special application.

Words for Rubbing and Bruising.

21. Proto-Aryan *mar*; Proto-Semitic מר, to rub, to bruise.

For the fullest discussions of the root *mar*, see M. Müller, Science of Language (Am. ed.), ii. p. 333 ff.; Pott, W. Wb. ii. 1. p. 522 ff. The radical notion is the one just given, as appears from a comparison of the multiudinous forms in which it is represented. In the European languages it comes out as *mal*, to grind, but in the Skr. *mar*, *mṛ-ṇấmi*, and Gr. μάρ-ν-αμαι, it means to fight, i.e. to act the "bruiser." How its use is shown by determinative forms we shall see hereafter. Whether *mar*, to die, is the same root, its sense being due to the intermediary notion of being worn down, we must leave an open question. In any case that meaning is secondary and unessential.—The Semitic מר means also to rub. The literal sense appears in Arab. مَرَّ, to rub (the udder in milking, cf. No. 23); in the Heb. מָרָה and מרא a figurative meaning is manifest: to be refractory, i.e. to rub against. The primary notion is more fully revealed in the forms with a guttural determinative: Heb. מרח, to rub, to bruise (cf. מָרוּחַ, Lev. xxi. 20), Arab. مَرَخَ, to rub or anoint with oil.

22. Proto-Aryan *mark*; Proto-Semitic מרק, to rub, stroke.

Cf. Skr. *març*, to stroke, touch, lay hold of; Lat. *mulc-eo*, to stroke; and perhaps Gr. μάρπ-τω, to seize upon, for μάρκ-τω (so Roth in Kuhn's Zeitschrift, xix. p. 222; cf. Curtius, p. 463).—מרק is represented in the Heb. מָרַק, to polish, or "rub up" metals, also to rub off, clean off; Syr. ܡܪܩ, Chald. מְרַק. In Arabic the *r* becomes *l* as in Latin; so مَلَقَ, to rub out, to wash off.

23. Proto-Aryan *marg* (*malg*); Proto-Semitic מלג, מרג, to rub, to press, to milk.

The root *marg* is very widely represented. Skr. *marj* means to rub, to make smooth or clean. Zend *marez* has the same force, but *maregh*, means to rove about (cf. Engl. "knock around"). Gr. ὀ-μόργ-νυμι, signifies to wipe off; ἀ-μοργ-ός, pressing out; μάργ-ος, roving about, wandering. In the European languages the root also means to milk, the *r* being replaced by *l*; so Gr. ἀ-μέλγ-ω, Lat. *mulg-eo*, Eng. *milk*, and in all the other dialects.—All of these meanings are illustrated in the Semitic מרג. The Heb. מרג means to rub hard, to press, as appears from מוֹרַג, a threshing-sledge (mod. Arab. *mauraj*; cf. Lat. *tribulum* < *tero*). From the sense of pressing comes that of urging (cf. the usage of the Lat. *urgeo*), or driving, in Chald. מְרַג. The Eth. መርገ, transfers the primary sense to that of rubbing on mortar or plastering (from the use of the trowel); while the Arabic, as in No. 22, and in the European *malk*, changes the *r* to *l*, and مَلَجَ means to milk. It is not here maintained that the agreement in the *l* sounds, or in the special sense of milking, is a proof that this very form in this very sense was common to the two families. This would be absurd. It only shows, in a way that is now becoming familiar to us, that the use of the fundamental root *marg* מרג, before the Aryo-Semitic schism, was such as to lend itself readily to this special application long ages afterwards.

24. Proto-Aryan *mard;* Proto-Semitic מרד, to bruise, press; to rub, to soften.

For the development of meaning in the root *mard*, see especially M. Müller, Science of Language, ii. p. 346 f.[1] The Skr. *mard, mṛd-nâ-ti; mrad, mrad-ate*, mean to press, also to rub to pieces. Hence the adj. *mṛd-u*, soft, i.e. impressible, with which cf. the Lat. *moll-is*, for *mold-vis*, and the Eccl. Slav., *mrad-u*, tender. The Gr. ἀ-μαλδ-ύνω, means to soften, or weaken; while our Engl. *melt* appears in Goth. *malt-an*, A. S. *melt-an*. Again, the Skr. *mṛd*, means earth or soil, as being pulverized — a word which reappears in Engl. *mold*. Finally, the Lat. *mord-eo*, to bite, combines in its signification the two ideas of pressing and rubbing or gnawing which are contained in the primitive root.—These various meanings emerge also in the Semitic מרד. The Heb. מרד, has the figurative sense of being refractory, rebellious, which we met with in No. 21. So the Syr. ܡܪܕ means to resist or struggle against. The Eth. መርደ gives the idea of assailing, attacking (cf. again *mar*, No. 21). In the Arabic, however, we find a more complete agreement with the Aryan signifi-

---

[1] The reader should be cautioned, however, against following Prof. Müller's ingenious observations beyond the forms that represent *mard* with phonological exactness.

RELATIONS OF THE ARYAN AND SEMITIC LANGUAGES. 139

cations. Besides having the sense of the Hebrew just given, مَرَدَ, means to soften (as bread or dates in water), to press with the teeth (used of children at the breast), while مَلَكَ means to soften in general, wherefore we have مَلَكَ, soft, مَلَكَ, softness, tenderness, with various allied derivatives, thus completing the analogy with the Aryan forms. With *mṛd* and *mold* may be compared the Eth. ዐፈርት, dust, earth, which, however we may try to account for its exact form,[1] is certainly developed from the root מר, with a form almost identical with the Proto-Aryan word.

25. Proto-Aryan *mars*; Proto-Semitic מרש, מרץ, to oppress, vex, obstruct.

The Skr. *marsh* means (1) to forget, (2) to endure patiently. The Lith. *mirsz-tu* means to forget. If we seek the missing link between these apparently unconnected ideas, it is found in the Goth. *marz-ian*, to hinder, vex. Forgetting is thus a mental obstruction.[2] The other Skr. sense, of enduring, is probably developed from an earlier application of the verb as neuter or passive : (1) to be vexed or oppressed ; (2) to suffer ; (3) to suffer patiently. The inflective form favors this view : *marsh*, *mṛsh-yati* (4. class ; see Whitney's Skr. Grammar, §§ 761, 762). Cf. the Latin *patior* (Fick, ii. p. 141), (1) to be vexed, (2) to suffer, (3) to suffer patiently — also a deponent verb, and of the same conjugational class as the Skr. word.—The Semitic root has not the special secondary sense of forgetting, but otherwise the parallel may be made complete. The primary notion of pressing, oppressing, is found in Heb. מָרַץ (as in 1 Kings ii. 8), Arab مَرَصَ, مَرَشَ, مَرَسَ, all of which have the sense of pressing or

[1] See Dillmann, Aeth. Gramm. p. 185; Lexicon Aeth. col. 167.
[2] A similar explanation is suggested by Pott (W. Wb. ii. 2, p. 447) for the Skr. sense of forgetting. If the word "*vyâ-marsh-a*, a rubbing out, erasure," cited by him were genuine, a solution just as good would be at hand. But it is not found in the Petersburg Dict. If an actual word, it is probably from the root *març* (No. 22), as a corrupted form.

squeezing, and Assyr. מרץ,[1] to use force, *marṣu*, harsh, violent. The idea of being oppressed is brought out in Assyr. *murṣ-u*, sickness,[2] Arab. مَرَضَ, to be weak, sick, conj. v. to show languor, while مُرْض, a disease of the mind, includes such mental ailments as languor and hesitation (see Freytag, iv. p. 169), thus furnishing a sort of analogy with the mental application of the Skr. *marsh*. Finally, the sense of obstructing appears in the very common Assyrian word *marṣ-u*, obstructive, impassable.

Thus in the two families we have a group of five pairs of roots of identical meanings and special applications comprised in *mar* (מר) and its secondaries. Nearly all the actual, as well as possible, manifestations of that root in the two systems will be found to be established in the foregoing presentation.

Words for Joining.

26. Proto-Aryan *gam;* Proto-Semitic גם, to join, to bring together.

There can be no reasonable doubt of the existence of *gam* as a Proto-Semitic root. For a succinct presentation of the argument see Curtius (5. ed.) p. 546 f. The words that establish it are Skr. *jâm-i*, related, connected (as children of one family), and as a noun, relationship; *vi-jâm-an*, coupled together, as the arms and legs; Latin *gem-ini*, twins, i.e. couples; Gr. γάμ-ος, marriage, γαμ-έω, to marry, (not a denominative, as is shown by ἔ-γημ-α); further, Skr. *jâm-âtar*, one related by marriage, a son-in-law, a husband, etc., just like Gr. γαμ-βρός; *jâm-â*, daughter-in-law; Latin *gen-er*, son-in-law, is evidently for *gem-er*, the *m* of *gem-ro* being replaced by *n*, perhaps through the influence of the following *r*, as Corssen thinks. The only verb-stem in which the root appears is, therefore, the Gr. γαμ-έω, unless γέμ-ω, to be full, is connected with it, in the sense of being pressed together, as Fick supposes (ii. p. 87). But the predicative root which yields all these forms can only mean to unite. A root *gam*,

---

[1] See Lenormant, Étude, etc., already cited, p. 78.
[2] For kindred Assyrian words, see Lenormant, op. cit., p. 82 ff.

to beget, nasalized like *gan*, from *ga* (γέ-γον-α: γε-γα-ώς) does not exist, and if it did it would not yield the forms that imply coupling. — The root גם has a large representation in Proto-Semitic, both in primary and in secondary forms. First we have the simple גם in Hebrew and Arabic. In the former it is not found as a verb-stem, but we find in Phenician the noun גֻּמֶּה (cited by Fürst, Wörterbuch s.v. גֵּם), assembly, community, while we have in Hebrew proper the conjunction גַּם, also, originally a substantive meaning union; cf. Arab. جَمَّ, to be many, to be heaped together, جَمَّة, an assembly. In Arabic, however, a more common word for uniting is جَمَعَ, being the same root with the post-determinative ע.

With the post-determinative ר we have גמר in all the dialects of the system in both verb and noun stems, meaning to bring all together, to complete. With other post-determinatives the same primary sense is directly or indirectly preserved.

Words for Stretching or Extending.

27. Proto-Aryan *tan;* Proto-Semitic תן to stretch, extend.

The Aryan root *tan* appears in Skr. *tan, tan-omi*, to stretch, strain; Zend. *tan*, to stretch out, spread out; Gr. τείνω for τεν-ιω, τι-ταίνω for τι-ταν-ιω, to stretch, extend; Lat. *ten-do*, to stretch, *ten-eo*, to hold, i.e. to keep on the strain; *tempto* (properly *ten-to*, according to Corssen), to try, or, primarily, as Curtius says, to stretch a thing till it fits; Goth. *than-yan;* A. S. *then-yan*, to extend. It is also found in many noun-stems in these and all the other Indo-European dialects, with kindred or derived meanings, in which the force of the primary idea is variously and vividly represented. This *tan* is really a nasalized form of *ta*, which appears as the stem before a consonant in Greek and Sanskrit. Thus *tan* in Skr. has the participle *ta-ta*, to stretch, and τείνω gives the aor. ἐ-τά-θην, while we also meet with the form τά-σις, a stretching, and τά-νυ-μαι, I stretch myself; cf. the note in Chap. IV. on nasal vowels in connection with the determinative *n*. — The Semitic תן shows itself most simply in the Heb. תָּנָה, to stretch, extend, and its antiquity is attested by the noun-stems ተን, extension, and ፈትን, a shoestring, in Ethiopic; and especially by the word for large serpent or sea-monster: Heb. and Chald. תַּנִּין; Arab. تِنِّينٌ, which is derived from תנן, just as the Lat. *regulus* is from *rego*, to stretch. With a predeterminative ו the idea of extension denoted by the simple root is transferred to time; hence the Arab. وَتَنَ, to be perpetual, and the obsolete Heb. יָתַן, which is to be presupposed for the noun אֵיתָן, perpetuity. With the predeterminative נ the idea of stretching becomes that of giving, or reaching forth.[1] So we have the Heb. נָתַן, to give, which appears also in Chaldee and Samaritan, and of which the Syr. ܢܬܠ is probably a corruption. The Assyr. נדן is the same word with *t* softened to *d*, according to a common change. In the Eth. ነተለ, however, the primary notion has apparently been transferred to the mental sphere, and the word means, in conj. IV. 1, to be busily engaged, assiduously occupied,[2] or, as we say, to have the mind on the strain, to be *in-tent*. The same root, תנ, with a vowel postdeterminative, appears in Heb. תִּנָּה, as well as in several of the Aramaic idioms, with the proper sense of rewarding.[3] As corresponding with the Aryan *ta* we may possibly have a relic of a Semitic תא or טא in the Arab. reduplicated form طَأْطَأَ, to incline downwards.

28. Proto-Aryan *nat* (*nit*); Proto-Semitic נט, נט, to stretch forward, incline.

[1] This transference of meaning is very common in language. It is manifest in the origin of the words *offer* and *proffer*, Lat. *praebeo* (= *prae-habeo*, to hold out), and even in the word *give* which is probably identical with the Lat. *habeo*, to hold. So also in the Skr. *prayacchâmi*, I offer, give, from the root *yam*, properly to stretch.

[2] See Dillman, Lex. Aethiop. col. 660, who, however, with apparent impropriety, connects the meaning with the idea of giving, and compares the Lat. expression: *se dedere*.

[3] Cf. the Lat. *dono* from *do*, or, as a still better illustration, the Germ. *dar-reichen*, to reach forth, present.

An Indo-European combination is given by Fick (I. 125). From the adducible examples there would seem to have been not only the root *nat*, but a degenerated form *nit*. The Skr. *náth* means to seek for help.[1] Comparing this with the Goth. *nath, nithan* (Teutonic *nâtha*), to support, help, and the Lat. *nit-or*, to strive after, to seek or gain support, it is evident that the primary meaning of the root is, to reach after, or stretch forwards. — On the Semitic side the Arab. نَصّ, and with a vowel determinative نَاصّ, to stretch out, lengthen, preserves the primary signification of the root; but the corresponding Heb. נָטָה, while yielding the same sense, means more generally to stretch or lean forwards, to incline. Again, Eth. ነጥዐ, with the post-determinative ע, means, primarily, to extend, stretch out, as the noun-stem ነጥዐ, a tent, implies, which is formed from it as Lat. *tentorium*, L. Lat. *tenta*, *tent*, came from *tendo*. But ነጥዐ also meant to stretch forward or incline, for its current sense is to flee or to be put to flight.[2] The proof is complete when we refer to the identical root in Syriac, ܢܛܐ, to incline, used specially of a scale of the balances.

29. Proto-Aryan *mad*; Proto-Semitic מד, to extend, to measure.

The root *ma* yields the common Indo-European words for measuring. In its undeveloped form it is found in Skr. *mâ*, to measure; Zend *mâ*, to measure, to produce; Gr. μέ-τρον, a measure; Lat. *me-tior*, to measure; Eccl. Slav. *mě-ra*, a measure. The secondary root *mad* is also Proto-Aryan. It appears in Lat. *mod-us* measure, and *mod-eror*, to keep in

---

[1] Pott's attempt (Wurzelwörterbuch, i. 576), to connect *náth* with *ní*, to lead, fails, because it begins at the wrong end of the train of ideas. The Skr. *nâtha*, means, a "leader," only because it first meant a protector, i e. one who is sought for help or support. As a neuter noun, *nâtha* means help or support.

[2] Just as the Lat. *fugio* is from the root *bhug*, to incline, bend, which also yields our English *bow*. The Arabic نَصّ, just cited, means also to flee; cf. Heb. נָטָה, 1 Sam. xiv. 7.

measure, *mod-ius* and Gr. μέδ-ιμνος, a bushel measure, and it takes the place of *ma* entirely in the Teutonic *mat* (Goth. *mitan*, Engl. *mete*). In the figurative sense of considering (cf. Germ. *ermessen*) we have it in Gr. μήδ-ομαι, to think on, μέδ-ομαι, to care for; while it is found also in the same sense in Keltic. The sense of measuring, then, is the prevailing notion attaching to these roots. That the primary idea was that of extension can, we think, be pretty clearly shown. In the first place the idea of measuring is not primitive; it is essentially a secondary and complex notion, implying a factitious comparison with an accepted standard: it must be expressed by the new application of a previously existing term. What, then, is it to measure? It is just to take the length, or rather the extent, of anything. Hence, when we come to examine in various languages the words for measuring whose etymology is accessible, we find that the radical notion is that of extending, in nearly every case.[1] In the second place, we have apparent secondary forms of the root *ma* which imply the notion of extending. There are in Indo-European apparently three roots, *mak*, *mag*, and *magh* (see Curtius, 5 ed. p. 328, No. 462), which had the sense referred to. These have given rise respectively to such representative words as the Gr. μακ-ρός, long; Lat. *mag-nus*, great, and Skr. *mah-ant*, great. These are most naturally to be connected with a root *ma*, having the general sense of extending.[2] In the third place, there is more direct evidence from the usage of the root *ma* itself. In Zend. it means to make, produce, and a similar sense is given by it in Sanskrit, when it is compounded with the prefix *nis*. But it is more significant still that the Proto-Aryan word for mother, *matar*, is from *ma*, and as it obviously means the producer, it shows how very early this meaning was attached to the root. Now,

[1] The Arab. كال is an exception. Like the equivalent Heb. כיל it primarily meant to hold or contain, and was thus applied to dry and liquid measure. This, of course, belongs to a later order of things.

[2] It is noteworthy that *mâ* is the stem of the Latin comparative *mâ-jor*, and that there is no final consonant in the stem of the Gaelic *mór* and Welsh *mawr*, great, which are undoubtedly hometymous.

we cannot very readily get the idea of producing from that of measuring, but we can very easily associate it, as well as the notion of measuring, with the idea of extending (cf. the Lat. *pro-duco*). — The root מא is preserved in the Arab. مَلا and مَلَى, to extend, spread out, and though it does not appear in other idioms in verb-stems without consonantal determinatives, it is probable that the Semitic word for hundred (Heb. מֵאָה) is derived from it. However this may be, there is no doubt that this fundamental expression occurs in many other forms. The most notable is the root מד, which appears as Proto-Semitic, not only in the simple form, but also with various determinatives, as מדח, מיד, מאר,[1] all having the notion of extending. The simple root מד had also, from early Semitic times, the sense of measuring, as appears from the Heb. מדד, to lengthen, to measure, as compared with the Arab. مُدّ, the name of a certain dry measure, from the root مَدَّ; cf. مُدْيُ, of like meaning. In the same way, as we have seen, the root *mad* yields the Lat. *mod-ius* and Gr. μέδ-ιμνα, and thus the analogy is completed with the root מד.

30. Proto-Aryan *rak̤*; Proto-Semitic, רך, to extend.

In the Indo-European sphere the two roots *rak̤*, *rag* lie side by side; each of them means, properly, to stretch, extend. Whether the form *rag* has been weakened from *rak̤*, according to the analogy of a multitude of roots in Greek (Curtius, p. 533 ff.), and occasional examples elsewhere, or whether they are equally autonomous, we do not need to attempt to determine. The root *rak̤*, in the sense of extending, seems to survive in the Zend *raç-ta*,[2] right, straight (as

---

[1] From this root comes the Assyr. *ma'adu*, great, and also, as Schrader has suggested (Keilinschriften u. d. Alte Test. p. 3) the Heb. מְאֹד, much, which has nothing to do with אור, to be strong.

[2] The ç here corresponds to an original *k̤*, as in Sanskrit, and not to *g*, which it represents, in place of an intermediate *z*, only before *m* and *n*. See Schleicher, Compendium, p. 186. The root is therefore *rak̤*, and not *raġ*. Pott, who brings it in under *rag* (Wurzelwörterbuch, iii. 593), admits that the sibilant looks suspicious. Fick (i. 406), combines with Lat. *rec-tus* (for *reg-tus*) without hesitation.

our word *right* is from the root *rag*). It also appears in the Skr. *raç-mi, raç-anâ*, a string, a thong, a measuring line, and probably in *râç-i*,[1] a large quantity. A weakened form of the same primitive root is perhaps traceable in the Lat. *por-ric-i-o*, to present, offer to the gods, which would stand to the root *rak̬* as *por-rig-o* does to *rag*,[2] which also has the sense of Lat. *pro-duco*. — The Semitic רך appears clearly in the form ארך, to extend. This is represented by Heb. אָרַךְ, to prolong; also to be long, or to delay; Arab. اَرَكَ, to delay, Syr. ܐܪܶܟ, to be long, delay; and in other Aramaic dialects. The Assyr. *arik*, long, with various other derivatives, presents the same root. רך, in this sense, seems also to have had another vowel predeterminative; for the Arabic وَرَكَ, means to delay, to linger,[3] while the same root in various Semitic idioms conveys the kindred notion of coming behind. It is most fully represented in Assyrian,[4] where we have *arku, arki, arka*, behind, *arka, arki*, after, *arkatu*, the hinder part of anything. The last-named word is the exact phonetic representation of the Heb. יְרֵכָה, which has the same meaning, and which also means the hinder part of the body; cf. Arab. وَرِكٌ, وَرْكٌ, and Heb. יָרֵךְ.

31. Proto-Aryan *rak*; Proto-Semitic רד, to dispose, arrange.

For the Indo-European root, see Fick I. 188 f., and cf. Pott III. 216 ff. (Nos. 1024, 1025). It is allowable to compare the Skr. *rac*, to arrange, compose, set right; Goth. *rak-nyan*,[5]

---

[1] It is a fancy of the Hindu grammarians that this is erroneously written for *râsi*. But no root *râs* or *ras* yields the proper sense.

[2] Cf. Corssen : Aussprache u. s. w. d. lat. Sprache, i. 500 f. He assumes a root *rik*, which he finds represented in many other words. Most of the combinations seem hazardous. The most plausible is that with O. High Germ. *rîh-an* (cf. Eng. *row*), to place in line.

[3] This root in Arabic also means to stand still. For the sense, may we not compare עמר, to stand, with the root מד, already discussed ?

[4] For a full discussion of the Assyrian words, see Lenormant: Etude sur quelques parties des syllabaires cunéiformes (Paris, 1876), p. 143 ff.

[5] This must be carefully distinguished from Eng. *reck-on*, A.S. *rec-nan*, which is from the root *rag*, to extend, direct.

to reckon, determine; Lith. *renk-ù*, to collect. — The Semitic root, like the preceding, is found with a light predeterminative: Heb. עָרַךְ, to set in line, arrange, adjust; Eth. ⵓⵥⵇ and ⵓⵥⵉ, to adjust, reconcile.[1]

Words for Bending or Curving.

32. Proto-Aryan *kap, kup;* Proto-Semitic כף, to bend, to curve.

Kap is represented in the Gr. κάμπ-τω, to bend, καμπ-ύλος, curved, and probably in Lat. *cap-erare*, to wrinkle. The Skr. *kamp*, which is undoubtedly the same root, to tremble, the expression being suggested by the curvature of trembling objects; *câp-a*, a bow, from the primitive form *kap*, preserves the earlier notion. The same notion is apparent in *kap-anâ*; Gr. κάμπ-η, a worm (cited by Fick, I. 39). — The Semitic כף has a very wide representation, and in its simplest form it appears in Heb. כָּפַף. Syr. ݒܦ; Chald. כַּף, to bend, to be curved; Arab. كَفَّ, to turn away or aside; while the Assyr. has it as a noun-stem in *kap-u*,[2] a hollow place. The apparent derivative כַּף, the palm, or hollow hand, is found throughout the system. With closely related meanings the root is also found with various determinatives in verb and noun stems that are surely Proto-Semitic.

33. Proto-Aryan *kmar;* Proto-Semitic כמר, to bend around.

The researches of Pictet[3] and of Pott (W. Wb. I. 503) have made highly probable the existence of a primitive root *kam*, with the sense of bending (comp. also Fick, I. 40). More certain, however, is the occurrence of a root *kmar*, with three

---

[1] There can be no doubt that the last two pairs of roots (Nos. 30, 31) were originally the same. The idea of arranging is a secondary one, and, according to a multitude of analogies, it is usually expressed by words that mean extend, etc., to put in line. So with our word *ar-range*, the Lat. *or-do* (cf. *or-ior*), *dispono, rec-tus*, our word *right, reck-on*, and a great number of hometymous words from the root *rag*. Indeed, the root אָרַךְ (No. 30), has also the sense of fitting, adjusting, in Hebrew, Talmudic, and Arabic.

[2] For examples of this word, see Norris, Assyrian Dictionary, p. 592 f.; cf. 516.

[3] Les origines indo-européennes (2d ed. 1877), ii. p. 277.

148 RELATIONS OF THE ARYAN AND SEMITIC LANGUAGES.

consonants. The Sanskrit has a root *kmar, kmarati*,[1] to be curved, and although the verb-stem does not emerge elsewhere, we find in Zend the noun *kamar-a*, a vault, and a girdle; cf. Gr. καμάρ-α, Lat. *camer-a*, a vault, and Lat. *cam-ur*, bent inwards (used of horns). It is possible, as Fick suggests, that the same stem appears in O. S. *himil* (Germ. *himmel*) as the vault of heaven. — The Semitic root is developed in precisely the same way. Cf. Eth. ቀመረ, to vault over, to make round, ቀመር, a vault, and an orb, with Chald. קְמַר, to gird; קְמוֹר, a girdle, Syr. ܩܡܪܐ.[2]

34. Proto-Aryan *ank* (*ak*); Proto-Semitic עק, to bend, curve.

The Indo-European has mostly the nasalized *ank* in stems from this root; but *ak* appears in some forms, and according to what was said on the subject of nasalization in Indo-European roots in Chap. IV., the primary sound may be represented by *ak*. Cf. Skr. *ac, anc*, to bend, *ak-a*, the curved bosom, and a kook; Zend *ak-a*, a clasp; Gr. ὄγκ-ος, a clasp, hook, ἀγκ-ών, the bent arm, ἀγκ-ύλος, bent, curved; Lat. *unc-us*, bent, and a hook; O. Irish *éc-ad*, a hook; Engl. *angle* in its two senses. — The Semitic root is not found in its simplest representation; but appears with a variety of determinatives, all of which reveal its primary force. Thus עקל (in verb or noun stems in Heb., Chald., Syr., and Arab.), to bend or twist; Eth. ዐቀመ, and Arab. عَقَّ, to bend, restrain, shut up; Syr. ܥܩܠ, Chald. עֲקַם, to twist, to turn; עקב, to bend, to arch, עקץ and עקש, to twist, all of which also are Proto-Semitic. Forms with other determinatives are found besides in the separate dialects. Moreover, the ancient roots עין and עקה give the idea of restraining, already adduced.

[1] This root, though not quotable in the literary language, is attested by the Dhâtupâtha; see the Petersburg Lexicon, s.v.

[2] This root is not borrowed from the Greek καμάρα, or from any Indo-European source. It is probable, however, that the Heb. כְּמָר, an idol-priest, through its Syriac equivalent, was derived from the Persian source above indicated; *kamrâ* was the girdle of the fire-worshippers.

WORDS EXPRESSIVE OF MOVEMENT.

35. Proto-Aryan *sad;* Proto-Semitic צד, to go.

The root *sad* has not a large extant representation in the Indo-European; but is well defined and well established. Cf. Skr. *sad,* to go; Gr. ὁδ-ός, a way, ὁδ-εύω, to walk, etc.; Eccl. Slav. *šĭd,* to go, *chod-ŭ* (χοdŭ), a course, *chod-iti,* to go, proceed. Other combinations made by Curtius (5 ed. p. 241, No. 381) must be regarded as hazardous; cf. Pott, IV. 712 f. (No. 1783). — The root צד, in its simplest representation, means to go away, to go aside;[1] Arab. صَدَّ, to turn aside; cf. Heb. צַד, a side. With indeterminative ע, Heb. צָעַד and Arab. صَعِدَ means to go up or go down, but also to proceed or march.[2] With internal vowel expansion we have צוּד, meaning to go after, to pursue; the Proto-Semitic word for hunting, found in all the dialects except the Ethiopic. The sense of lying in wait, ascribed by Gesenius to this root as its primary meaning, is naturally secondary. It seems also probable that through the postdeterminative ק, the root צדק, the ancient and universal term for righteousness, meant primarily, to go straight, or right on.

36. Proto-Aryan *sar;* Proto-Semitic שר, to go, to move quickly.

The root *sar* is found in Skr. *sar,* to go, to flow; Zend *har,* to go; Gr. ἄλλ-ομαι, to spring, ἄλ-σις, springing, etc., ὁρ-μή, impulse; Lat. *sal-io,* to leap, and many other Indo-European forms. — שר is seen in Arab. سَارَ, Med. Ye, to go, to walk, to journey; سَارَ, Med. Waw, to go up, to leap upon; Heb. שׁוּר, to travel, to go around; Chald. שְׁוַר, Syr. ܫܘܪ, to leap upon or forward. These forms arise from internal

---

[1] That the verb is not a denominative from צד, a side, is proved from the fact that the latter is only Hebrew, while the former is Proto-Semitic. The Syr. ܨܝܕ, with, among, is, of course, not connected with צד.

[2] Cf. the uses of Latin *scando,* and its compounds; also the Proto-Aryan *skand* (Fick, i. 232), in which all the above meanings are exemplified.

vowel expansion. The simplest form is apparently preserved in Eth. ﬁ⟋⟋, to leap, to rush upon (in the Amharic dialect the same root means to be carried along); while with the determinative ט we find Arab. سَرَعَ, to go swiftly; Syr. ܫܪܥ, to slip down. The agreement between the Aryan and Semitic roots in both general and special meanings should be well noted.

37. Proto-Aryan *ragh*; Proto-Semitic רג, to move quickly.

For the various representations of the root *ragh* Fick, I. p. 190, may be compared with Curtius, p. 192 (No. 168). We shall cite a few cases in which it undoubtedly appears: Skr. *rañh* (= *rah* = *ragh*) and *rangh* (= *ragh*), to run, to hasten; *langh*, to spring up or over; *rangh-as*, *rañh-as*, *rah-as*, swiftness, haste; *lagh-u* and *ragh-u*, quick, small; Gr. ἐ-λαχ-ύς, small; Lat. *lev-is*, light, for *legv-is*; Eccl. Slav. *lig-uku*, light; Goth. *leih-tas* = Eng. *light*; O. Irish, *ling-im*, I leap, and the common Teutonic root *lang-an*, to go forward, hasten. — The root רג appears in Arab. رَجَّ, to move quickly, to tremble; Syr. ܪܓ, to long after, to desire = Chald. רָג.[1] With a postdeterminative ז, we have רגז (Heb., Aram., and Arabic), combining the notions of trembling and being angry. With postdeterminative ל, the root, in the form רגל, means to run, to go about: cf. Heb. רָגַל, to move about; Syr. ܪܓܠ, to lead, ܪܓܠܐ, a torrent; thence also a Proto-Semitic word for foot (found in Heb., Syr., Chald., Arabic, and some minor dialects), Heb. רֶגֶל.[2]

38. Proto-Aryan *di* (*da*); Proto-Semitic די (רי), to move swiftly, to fly.

The root *di* shows itself in Skr. *di* and *dî*, to hasten, to fly; Gr. δί-ω, to flee, to hasten, δί-εμαι, to speed away, δι-νός, a

---

[1] For the connection of ideas, cf. Lat. *cupio*, which is hometymous with Skr. *kup*, to move quickly, to be angry; see Pott, W.Wb. v. 91. Our word to *long* for and the Germ. *er-lang-en*, are from the root under discussion.

[2] So our word *foot*, representing the Proto-Aryan term, is from the root *pad*, to go.

whirling, δίνω, etc., to whirl; O. Irish dí-an, swift. That there was another, perhaps earlier, form da, as Fick (IV. 106) suggests, seems probable enough from the Gr. δο-νέω, to shake, to drive about. — The root דא is seen in Heb. דָּאָה, to fly swiftly (see especially Deut. xxviii. 49; Ps. xviii. 11); cf. Arab. دَاْدَ, to run swiftly, also to roll about. Hence, or from a cognate די, we have the Heb. דַּיָּה; Chald. דַּיָּא; Syr. ܕܰܝܬܳܐ, the name of a bird of prey, so called from its swift flight.

39. Proto-Aryan *tal*; Proto-Semitic תל, to raise, to weigh.

The root *tal* has a very wide distribution. For a very satisfactory discussion of the history and mode of its development, see Curtius, p. 220 f. (No. 236); cf. Fick, I. 94; Pott, II. 304–314 (No. 442). In Greek the fundamental form has been retained, though it also appears as *tel* and *tol*. Thus we have, with other forms, τλ-άω, for ταλ-άω, to bear, τάλ-ας, enduring, wretched, τάλ-αντον, a balance, weight, τέλ-λω, to rise, and also to raise upon (cf. ἀνατέλλω and ἐπιτέλλω), τόλ-μα, endurance, daring. In Sanskrit the degenerated form *tul* alone appears: *tul*, to lift up, weigh, *tul-â*, balance. In Latin the ground-form is *tol*, from which *tul* comes by weakening: *toll-o*, *tul-i*, *tol-erare*. In Teutonic the root comes out as *thul*; Goth. *thul-a*, I endure (cf. Germ. *dul-den*; Scottish *thole*; Eng. *thole-pins*). In Eccl. Slavonic we find *tul-ŭ* a quiver; and in Irish *tal-laim*, I take away. The occurrence of this root throughout the Indo-European system is one of the strongest evidences of the existence of a Proto-Aryan *l*. Cf. our remarks on that point under the subject of comparative phonology. — The Semitic תל agrees with *tal* not only in the primary, but also in most of the secondary meanings. In the simplest inflective form the Heb. תָּלַל means to raise, also to heap up; cf. Chald. תְּלִיל, elevated; Assyr. *tal-lu*, exaltation; Arab. مُنتَصِب, erect. From this root we have the word for mound or heap: Heb. and Chald. תֵּל; Syr. ܬܶܠܳܐ; Arab. تَلّ; Assyr. *tul*. The same root has the sense of suspending,[1] hanging up; hence in Heb. תַּלְתַּלִּים, the pendulous leaves of the palm. A like meaning is found in חלה, which is the same root with a post-determinative vowel, and appears in Heb., Chald., and Syriac, though the primary sense of lifting up comes out also in Syriac. In Arabic and Ethiopic the associated idea of adhering to is expressed by this form.[2] The vitality of the root is further seen in the Arab. جَلَا, to rise up, become prominent, طَلَعَ, to ascend, to rise (used of the sun and stars); conj. II., to raise up. The Assyr. נשל[3] derives its meaning of weighing from the same root with predeterminative נ.

Words indicating Position.

40. Proto-Aryan *sad*; Proto-Semitic סד, to sit, to be situated.

For the familiar root *sad* cf. the Skr. *sad*, to sit; Lat. *sed-eo*; Teutonic *sat* (Goth. *sit-an*; Engl. *sit*; cf. Goth. causative *sat-yan*; Engl. *set*), and corresponding terms in Slavonic and Celtic. The Gr. ἑδ, for σεδ, is transitive; cf. εἷ-σα, for ε-σεδ-σα, I set, ἕζ-ομαι, for σεδ-ιομαι, I sit = Germ. *ich setze mich*. The causative form *sad-aya* is also Proto-Aryan, and a large number of primary noun-stems in all the dialects preserve the ancient root. The force of the causative verbs throughout shows that the word meant first not to sit, but to be situated or placed. — The Semitic סד appears mostly as causative or transitive with the predeterminate י; so Heb. יָסַד, to place, to lay a foundation, to set in order = Chald. יְסַד; Arab. وَسَّدَ, with a specialized meaning, to set a pillow; Assyr. *isid*,[4] a foundation; cf. Heb. יָסוֹר, etc. That

---

[1] So in Greek τάλ-αρος, a basket, and τελ-αμών, a supporting strap, from the root *tal*. These as well as the words for weighing, above cited, have their meaning from the sense of suspending.

[2] Cf. the Germ. *an-hangen*, to cling, adhere.

[3] It should be mentioned that in Hebrew, Chaldee, and Syriac the same root means to raise, and to be heavy; the additional meaning in Assyrian well illustrates the Greek and Sanskrit usage.

[4] See Norris, Assyr. Dict. (ii.), p. 495, for sufficient examples.

the root סר was primarily intransitive is clear from the Arab. سَلَّ, to be placed, to be in the way, to obstruct; cf. Heb. סַר; Chald. סָרְיָא; Syr. ܣܳܪܳܐ, a block; while the Heb. סוֹד, an assembly (cf. Lat. *consessus*) has as its most probable etymon an obsolete verb סָדַד or סוּד, meaning to sit. With a postdeterminative ר we find סדר (Heb., Chald., and Syriac), meaning to set in order, like the Heb. יָסַד in one of its applications.

41. Proto-Aryan *as, âs*; Proto-Semitic אש, to sit, to remain.

Cf. No. 53. For discussion of the root *âs* see Pott, W. Wb. II. 2. 299–302 (No. 683); Curtius, p. 379 f. (No. 568). The following forms clearly represent it: Skr. *âs*, to sit, dwell, remain; Zend *âh*, to sit, to remain; Gr. ἧ-μαι, for ἧσ-μαι, I sit. Very probable derivations are, Lat. *â-nus*, for *as-nus*, the fundament, and Lith. *as-là*, floor, ground. — The Semitic אש does not seem to be retained as a verb-stem, except in denominatives, but its existence in the sense indicated is shown in many noun-stems. Cf. Arab. أسّ and أسّ, a foundation, also anything that remains or abides; أسس, the foundation of a house = Assyr. *asas-u, uss-u*, foundation; Heb. אָשִׁישׁ. Hence Arab. أسّس, Assyr. *asas-u*, to lay a foundation. The root also comes out in אשה with similar meanings in Heb. and Arabic. From these instances it is clear that, as in the Proto-Aryan *âs*, the root אש meant originally to be placed, to remain.

42. Proto-Aryan *man*; Proto-Semitic מן, to stay, to be fixed.

For a full exhibition of the words that spring from the root *man* see Pott, W. Wb. II. 2, 118 ff. (No. 607). The discussion of Curtius, p. 311 ff. (No. 429), is complicated by the identification of this root with *man*, to think. This combination, which is maintained by leading Indo-European etymologists, is of no significance for our present business, inasmuch as *man*, to remain, is an independent Proto-Aryan root.¹ We cite Zend and Old Persian *man*, to remain ; Mod. Persian *mán*, to remain, also abiding, eternal ; Gr. μέν-ω, 1. to stand fast, to endure ; 2. transitively, await, expect ; μί-μν-ω, to remain, await ; Lat. *man-eo*, to remain, also to wait for. Such noun-stems as Gr. μον-ή and Lat. *man-sio* show well the inherent notion of the root. — Precisely the same primary sense appears in the various representations of the Semitic מן. With the lightest predeterminate א the root אמן, widely represented in verb and noun stems in all the dialects, means to be fixed, firm, enduring, and in causative uses and forms, to make firm, establish. The figurative sense of enduring, abiding, comes out in all the dialects as clearly and fully as it appears in the root *man*. Thus the simplest abstract expression of the root is Heb. אֱמֶת, for אֲמֶנֶת. Assyr. *amat-u;* Arab. اَمْنٌ ; Eth. ኣመን, truth, fidelity, religion, i.e. what is fixed and abiding. This figurative use is almost the exclusive one in some of the dialects ; but the primary physical notion is exhibited in all. With the predeterminative ע the Arab. عَمَنَ means to stand still, to remain in a place. This last form, though not certainly Proto-Semitic, shows the presence and force of the ancient root, with its meaning as above given.

Words for Shutting or Enclosing.

43. Proto-Aryan *klu;* Proto-Semitic כלא, to shut, enclose.

The Indo-European root is not found in the Indo-Eranian division, but it appears in every other branch of the family, and must have a Proto-Aryan origin. For its manifestations see Pott, W. Wb. I. 684 ff. (No. 227) ; Curtius, p. 149 f. (No.

¹ The identity of these two roots is nothing more than a brilliant hypothesis. No apt analogy for the etymological association of the ideas is at hand. Something more is needed than a mere plausible connection of the notions expressed. And the association is nothing more than plausible. The intermediary idea is given by Pott, for example, as that of expecting or waiting in meditation. But it will be found that in all the cases where the root shows the two meanings of expecting and remaining, the latter is primary, the former secondary. So with *manere*, μένω, μίμνω. In any case *man*, to remain, and *man*, to think, should be treated as separate roots.

59); Fick, I. 541. The most significant representations are found in Gr. κλη-ίς, κλείς, for κλεϜ-ις, a key, κλείω, for κλεϜ-ίω, to shut, κλοι-ός, a collar, κλεῖ-θρον, a bolt or bar; Lat. *clâv-is*, a key, *clâv-us*, a nail (as a fastener), *clau-do*, to shut; O. Irish *clú-i*, nails; Lith. *kliův-ù*, to fasten on, attach. Whether the Old High Germ. *sliu-zan*, for *skliu-z-an*, to shut (whence Germ. *schliessen*, *schloss*, etc.; cf. Engl. *sluice*, *slat*, *slot*), belongs here is doubtful; but its affinity would not prove, as Curtius imagines, that the root was primarily *sklu*. See our remarks on the prothetic *s* in the discussion of the morphology of Aryan roots. — The Semitic כלא is represented by Heb. כָּלָא, to shut, enclose, כֶּלֶא, a prison; Chald. כְּלָא; Syr. ܟܠܐ, to shut, ܟܠܐ, a bolt; Eth. ከልአ, to shut out, prohibit; Arab. كلأ, to guard, watch; Assyr. כלא,[1] to hold back, to refuse. The root has also the secondary sense of shutting out, separating,[2] as appears from the Heb. כִּלְאַיִם, different species, with hometymous words in Ethiopic and Arabic. A great number of Semitic forms point to a simpler root, כל, represented in all the dialects, with the general sense of including, holding, containing. It should also be observed that the Aryan root *klu* has not the physiognomy of an ultimate root.

Words for Guarding against or Fearing.

44. Proto-Aryan *var*; Proto-Semitic רו, to guard against, to fear.

The root *var* may be traced through its various manifestations in its treatment by Pott, W. Wb. II. 1. 552–597 (No. 512); Fick, I. 211; Curtius, p. 346 f. (No. 501), and p. 550 (No. 660). We shall cite only a few of the many cases in which the root appears, according to the judgment of these and other leading etymologists. These instances will be found to be the most truly representative: Skr. *var*, to cover, protect, ward off; *vâr-a*, *var-âtha*, defence; Zend *apa-var*, to

---

[1] E.g. *ik-lu-u*, Inscr. of Khorsabad (ed. Oppert), lines 28, 69, 113, and *ik-la-a*, lines 79, 122.

[2] Cf. *ex-cludo*, *dis-cludo*, and διᾰ-κλείω.

ward off, hold back, *var-atha*, defence; Gr. ὄρ-ομαι, for Fορ-ομαι, to keep watch, οὖ-ρος, a sentinel, φρου-ρά, for πρυ-Fορ-a, a guard, ὦρ-α, care, apprehension, ὡρ-άω, to see; Lat. *ver-eor*, to fear, *ver-êcundus*, modest, i.e. diffident, apprehensive; Goth. *var-ian*, to keep off, *var-as*, careful; O. High Germ. *wâr-a*, care, regard (cf. Engl. *war-y, ware, ward, a-ware*). — The Semitic root unites in the most signal manner the two meanings of guarding and fearing, indicated by the Aryan *var*. We first call attention to the Arab. وَرَى, to repel, hinder. Comparing this with the Eth. ቀጸለ, an apron, from the corresponding obsolete root ዐጸለ, it is clear that the primary meaning was to keep off, to guard against. Now the same root in Hebrew is יָרֵא, meaning to fear, which completes the parallel. If further assurance is needed, we may cite the Arab. وَرِع, وَرَع, and وَرَع, which is the same root יר with post-determinative ע, and means to be afraid of, to keep away from, وَرِع, pious, God-fearing (cf. Lat. *re-verens*). Its equivalent, the Heb. יָרַע, means to tremble, i.e. to quake with fear (Isa. xv. 4). No two related words in different branches of the Indo-European family show more striking correspondences in meaning than do the root *var* and יר.

Words for Binding together.

45. Proto-Aryan *sar*; Proto-Semitic סר, צר, to bind together.

For the root *sar* see especially Curtius, p. 353 f. (No. 518), and the references to Kuhn's Zeitschrift there given. We cite the following forms: Skr. *sar-at*,[1] a thread; Gr. ὅρ-μος, for σόρ-μος, a collar, necklace, ὁρ-μαθός, a string, or chain, εἴρ-ω, to tie, to bind, εἰρ-μός, a fastening, εἴρ-ερος, bondage; Lat. *ser-o*, to string, to tie, *ser-a*, a bolt (fastener), *ser-ies*, a

---

[1] See the Petersburg Dictionary, s.v. The word is not cited there from current literature, but from a native lexicon.

series, *ser-tum*, a garland ; O. Norse *sör-vi*, a collar; Lith. *ser-is*, a thread. — The Semitic סר has properly the sense of holding together firmly. With predeterminative א it yields the Heb. אסר; Syr. אֶסַר; Arab. أَسَرَ; Eth. አስረ and አሠረ, to bind, with many hometymous noun-stems ; for the Assyrian we may compare *esir-u*,[1] a band. With another predeterminative, the Heb. יָסַר, to punish, chasten, obviously meant at first to bind.[2] The root צר, with a like primary force, appears in Heb. צָרַר; Arab. صَرَّ; Syr. צַר, Chald. צר, all meaning to bind together. The same root, צר, reveals the same meaning in many developed forms ; the examples just given will, however, suffice for our purpose.

Words for Pressing and Crushing.

46. Proto-Aryan *mak*; Proto-Semitic מך, to press, to crush.

Certain of the ideas expressed by this pair of roots agree with some conveyed by the group meaning to rub, to bruise (Nos. 21–26), though the fundamental notions are different. For the root *mak*, cf. Skr. *mac*,[3] with the bye-form *manc*, to crush ; Gr. root μαγ, for μακ, in μάσσω (= μαγ-ιω), to knead, μαγ-εύς, a baker, μάγ-μα, etc., dough, bread; Lat. *mac-er*, lean, meagre (i.e. pressed out), *mâc-erare*, to macerate, *mâc-eria*, a clay wall (as kneaded or pressed together); Lith. *mìnk-au*, I knead ; Eccl. Slav. *mak-a*, flour. Curtius, in his discussion of the Greek root (p. 356 : No. 455), cites with approval the conjecture that the Lat. *maxilla*, jawbone, or crusher, belongs here also. — The Proto-Semitic מך is shown in Heb. מָכַךְ, to sink (to be pressed down) ; and while the Chald. מְכַךְ preserves the transitive meaning to press down, part. מְכִיךְ, humbled, afflicted, the developed form מָאַךְ exhibits the intransitive sense, answering to Heb. מָכַךְ. The Arab. مَكَّ, again, has figurative applications : to diminish,

---

[1] The cuneiform sign indicated by *e* stands often for א as well as for ע.
[2] Cf. the Indo-European *dam*, to subdue, as developed from *da*, to bind ; Lat. *stringo* in Virgil, Aen. 9. 294 ; Germ. *bändigen*.
[3] Attested by Hindu lexicographers ; see the Petersburg Dictionary.

to consume, and in conj. v. to oppress a debtor. With indeterminative ע the Heb. מָעַךְ means to press and to crush (cf. 1 Sam. xxvi. 7 and Ezek. xxv. 3 with Lev. xxii. 24); and Arab. مَعَكَ means to rub and, as the derivations show, to crush small. The Chald. מְעַךְ has a meaning similar to that of the Hebrew; and as the root מך, with the secondary מְעַךְ, run a perfectly parallel course through Hebrew, Aramaic, and Arabic, they are plainly Proto-Semitic in the sense indicated.

WORDS FOR CARVING OR GRAVING.

47. Proto-Aryan *grap, glup*; Proto-Semitic גלב, to carve, to grave.

For these Aryan roots cf. Curtius, p. 178, 180 (Nos. 134, 138), with Fick, I. 574. The root *grap* is seen in the Gr. γράφ-ω, for γράπ-ω, to cut into (as in Iliad 17, 599), to write;[1] A. S. *ceorf-an*; Swed. *karf-va*; Engl. *carve*. The root *glup* appears in Gr. γλύφ-ω, for γλύπ-ω, to grave, γλύφ-ανος, a graving tool, γλυφ-ή, carved work, γλυπ-τής, a sculptor; A. S. *cleof-an*, to hew; Engl. *cleave*. The *f* in the primary Teutonic forms shows that the final letter was originally *p*. The A. S. *graf-an*; Engl. *grave*, may possibly be from the root *grap*, with *g* exceptionally retained; but this is by no means certain. We cannot agree with Curtius in comparing the Lat. *glub-o*, to peel off, with γλύφ-ω. These are probably related, but not identical. The use of *grap* and *glup*, with their train of allied words in the widely separated Greek and Teutonic, is very strong evidence that they are Proto-Aryan. — The Semitic גלב is represented in Chald. גְּלַב, frequent in the Targums; Syr. ܓܠܒ, Eth. ገለፈ, to carve, to grave, which is common in verb and noun stems relating to sculpture. The Arab. جَلَفَ means to cut off, and especially to peel off (cf. the use of *glubo* just mentioned). In

---

[1] So terms for writing are made generally from such words; cf. Engl. *write*, with Germ. *ritzen*; and the Lat. *scribo* is from a root allied to *grap* with prothetic *s* and just as *sculpo* is related to *glup*.

regard to the roots here combined it should be observed that neither of them is secondary in its origin; the evidence of their primary identity is strengthened from the consideration that to all appearance they are ultimate roots.

WORDS FOR PIERCING, INFIXING.

48. ? Proto-Aryan *smar;* Proto-Semitic שמר, to pierce, infix.

All leading etymologists hold to the originality of the *s* in the root *smar*. For the forms cf. Pott, W.Wb. v. 713 ff. (No. 550); Fick, I. 254; Curtius, p. 330 (No. 466). The following forms will show that the current Indo-European sense of the root is to hold in mind; Skr. *smar*, to remember, keep in mind; Zend *mar*, of like meaning; Lat. *me-mor*, mindful, etc.; Gr. μέρ-ιμνα, anxiety, μέρ-μερ-ος, memorable, μάρ-τυρ, a witness, etc. The idea of remembering or keeping in mind is, of course, secondary. It remains to be seen what the primary notion was. This cannot be learned from the form of the root *smar* itself; but perhaps it is legitimate to try to get it from other sources. Let us look at the secondary root *smard*, formed through the determinative *d*. This is seen in A. S. *smeart-an*, to feel stinging pain; Engl. *smart;* cf. Germ. *schmerz;* Gr. σμερδ-αλέος, σμερδ-νός, terrible, frightful; Zend *a-hmars-ta*, for *a-smard-ta*, not bitten or gnawed [1] (cited by Pott, W. Wb. v. 540). This last form is the key to the meaning of the other words: *smard* meant (1) to pierce, and (2) to pierce or sting the soul, just as Lat. *pungo* means (1) to pierce, and (2) to vex or grieve. The primary *smar* would then mean (1) to pierce, (2) to pierce or infix in the mind, to remember. This is in accordance with the analogy of many similar terms in other languages. Thus the familiar Semitic root צמר meant (1) to pierce, (2) to pierce or infix in the mind, to remember. The Heb. שָׁמַר, as we shall presently show, means (1) to pierce, (2) to keep in mind, to watch. Cf. also Arab. خَذَقَ, to cut, to pierce,

---

[1] Fick assigns here the Lat. *mord-eo*, to bite; but see No. 24.

to commit to memory; قَصَّ, to cut, conj. v. to keep in memory. The root *smar*, then, according to the best lights, meant first to pierce. — That סמר and שמר mean to pierce, to infix, is apparent from the following examples: Heb. מַסְמֵר; Chald. מַסְמְרָא; Arab. مِسْمَار, a nail; Chald. סְמַר; Arab. سمر, conj. II., to fasten with nails. Now the Heb. שָׁמִיר means a thorn, and Arab. سَمُر, thorns, especially "spina Egyptiaca"; Heb. שָׁמִיר and Assyr. *semir-u* also meaning a diamond. The Heb. שָׁמַר, and Chald. סְמַר mean to keep in mind, to watch, i.e. obviously, to pierce, or fix in the mind. The analogy is thus completed with the root *smar*.

WORDS FOR WETTING OR POURING OUT.

49. Proto-Aryan *sak* (*sik*); Proto-Semitic שק, to moisten, pour out.

For the Indo-European forms see Pott, W. Wb. v. 331–334 (No. 1069); Curtius, p. 137 (No. 24 *b*); Fick, I. 229. The following forms from *sik* are representative: Skr. *sic*, to moisten, sprinkle, pour out, *sek-a*, *sec-ana*, a sprinkling, etc.; Gr. ἰκ-μάς, moisture, ἴκ-μιος, moist, etc., also ἴχ-ωρ, divine blood; O. High Germ. *sîh-an* (cf. Germ. *seih-en*), to strain, filter, *seich*, wine; Eccl. Slav. *sĭc-ati*, to make water. Fick (cf. IV. 56) calls attention to Lith. *sunk-iu*, to filter; Eccl. Slav. *sok-ŭ*, juice; Lat. *sang-uis*, blood, as indicating the existence of an earlier root *sak*, from which *sik* arose through weakening. — For Semitic forms cf. Arab. سَقَى, to moisten, water, pour out water; Eth. ፈቀፐ, to water. In Hebrew, Aram., and Assyrian the corresponding verbs mean to be moist, to drink in, and in the causal forms, to water, give to drink. The notion of drinking is, of course, secondary. It is not found at all in Ethiopic, and is subordinate in Arabic, as it does not appear in any of the sixteen derivative nouns.

RELATIONS OF THE ARYAN AND SEMITIC LANGUAGES. 161

WORDS DENOTING COLD.

50. Proto-Aryan *ḳar;* Proto-Semitic קר, to be cold, to freeze.

The root *ḳar* is established by Fick, I. 57. Cf. Skr. *çi-çir-a*, cold (as noun and adjective); Zend *çar-eta*, cold; Lith. *szal-u*, to freeze, *szal-nà*, hoar-frost, also *szar-mà*. The A. S. and Icelandic *hrîm;* Engl. *rime*, probably contains the same root. — For the root קר cf. Arab. قَرَّ, to be cold; Eth. ቀዝዝ, to be cold; Syr. ܩܪ, to become cool (cf. Chald. אִתְקְרִיר, to cool ones self). It appears also in many noun-stems in all of these dialects, as well as in Heb. קַר, cold (adj.), and קֹר, cold (noun), etc. It is not remarkable that we should find an Aryo-Semitic word for cold, when we find so many for the action of fire (Nos. 1–4).

WORDS FOR THINKING.

51. Proto-Aryan *man;* Proto-Semitic מן, to think (to measure).

The familiar root *man* in Indo-European means, predominantly, to think. The following are a few of the numerous forms that represent it: Skr. *man;* Zend *man*, to think, suppose; Gr. μέν-ος, spirit, disposition, μαίν-ω, for μαν-ιω, to rave, μάν-τις, a seer; Lat. *men-s*, mind, etc., *men-tior*, to lie (i.e. to devise); Goth. *ga-mun-an*, to think of; A. S. *ge-mun-an*, remember, *man-ian*, to remind, *maen-an*, to wish = Engl. *mean;* Lith. *min-iù*, to think of; O. Irish *men-me*, mind. The primary meaning is to measure, as all etymologists agree, and it is clearly a secondary from *ma*[1] (No. 29). In some words for measuring, the root *man* actually appears, as in Lat. *men-sus*, participle of *me-tior*, *men-sa*, a table, *im-man-is*, immense. — For the sense of thinking in the root מן cf. the form with indeterminative א, Arab. مَأَنَ, to care

---

[1] The root *ma* also means to think, as in Skr. *mâ-ti*, thought, Gr. μῆ-τις, and in Gr. μέ-μα-α, etc., to wish for; *man* in this case does not arise through the nasalization of the vowel.

for, to be aware of; conj. II. and III. to consider, cogitate. Turning to the Proto-Semitic form with inner vowel expansion, we find the Eth. መየነ, in conj. III. 2, means (1) to devise means, in general, and (2) to devise cunningly, fraudulently. The first meaning is, of course, the primary one. The corresponding Arab. مَانَ, mid. Ye, retains the secondary sense of the Ethiopic, and means, to use deceit, to lie (cf. the use of Lat. *mentior*); but with mid. Waw it corresponds to the primary sense of the Ethiopic and to the sense of مَانَ, above cited, meaning to care for, provide for. But the same root exists in Heb. תְּמוּנָה, likeness, image, form, and מִין, a species, and is then evidently used to express the idea of a mental conception or image transferred to sensible objects[1] (cf. the various uses of the Gr. ἰδέα). The notion of thinking is thus shown to be Proto-Semitic. If the primary notion of the root is sought for, it seems more than probable that it is to be found in those common Semitic words from the root מן which convey the fundamental idea of measuring. For example, the Heb. מנה; Arab. مَنَى means to measure out, allot (cf. Germ. *ermessen*), and the same root in all the dialects means to number, while the Arab. مَنًا means a definite measure or weight. Derivations and kindred roots illustrate the same general signification. The Aryan and Semitic roots are thus shown to be completely in accord.

Words for Knowing.

52. Proto-Aryan *vid*; Proto-Semitic יד, to know.

The root *vid* is one of the most familiar of the whole Indo-European stock. The citation of the following forms will suffice: Skr. *vid*, perf. *ved-a*, I know, *vid*, to find; Gr. ἰδ-εῖν, for Ϝιδ-εῖν, to see, οἶ-δα, for Ϝοῖ-δα, I know = Skr. *veda*,

---

[1] Hence, in Job iv. 16, תְּמוּנָה is expressively employed for a form appearing in visions of the night. Gesenius' association of these words with the Arabic sense of deceiving, is as though one should derive *species* from *specious*, or *fingo* from *feign*.

RELATIONS OF THE ARYAN AND SEMITIC LANGUAGES. 163

iδ-éa, a conception, etc.; Lat. *vid-ere*, to see, etc.; Goth. *vait*, I know = Skr. *ved-a*; cf. Engl. *wit, wot, wit-ness*; Eccl. Slav. *vid-ěti*, to see, *věd-ěti*, to know; Old Prussian *vaid-imai*, we know. The idea of knowing predominates in the system as a whole, but in some of the dialects the notion of seeing prevails; and it may be true, as Curtius says (p. 101, Engl. transl. of 4. ed., p. 124), that the fundamental expression was that of a seeing which apprehended and discovered. This fact, however, has no direct bearing upon the validity of our combination; for the sense of knowing evidently goes back to early Proto-Aryan times. — The Semitic root is no less ancient, as it is found in all the great divisions of the family. It sometimes expresses the idea of observing, though the physical notion of seeing is not found. We cite the following verbal forms: Heb. יָדַע; Chald. יְדַע; Syr. ܝܕܥ; Assyr. *id-u*, to know; Eth. ፐፀዐ, conj. II. 1, to make known, etc. That the first radical was originally ו appears from the Heb. הִתְוַדַּע in the Hithpael, and the Assyrian forms[1] are rightly assigned to the Assyr. 'אפ, or original 'פו class, by leading authorities. The Ethiopic ፐ in the place of the first radical is probably an early dialectic variation. That the third radical, ע, is merely a determinative is made plain from the fact that the fundamental notion is expressed also by the Proto-Semitic root ודה. This in the causative forms, Heb. הוֹדָה; Syr. ܐܘܕܝ; Chald. אוֹדִי, cf. Arab. وَدَىٰ, conj. X., means both to celebrate and to confess,[2] i.e. to make known.

---

[1] See Lenormant, Etude sur quelques parties des syllabaires cunéiformes, p. 171; Schrader, Keilinschriften u.d. alte Test. p. 223.

[2] These meanings can be best explained on the hypothesis of a connection between ודה and ידע. The common way of treating them is to make them causatives of the homophonous root ודה, to throw. But this does not explain them at all suitably. Nor is the attempt more successful (Gesenius's Hebrew Handwörterbuch, 8th ed. by Mühlau and Volck), to associate ידע with the Arab. وَدَىٰ, to place. The connection is not obvious; and since the root in the sense of knowing is absent from the Arabic only of all the dialects, and in the sense of placing is found only in Arabic, the combination shows bad etymologizing.

The root רי is thus shown to be as old and independent as the root *vid*, and it is worthy of attention that the meanings coincide precisely. The application of both roots is almost exclusively to mental, not to physical apprehension. They do not signify to be acquainted with, but to know within the strict sphere of self-consciousness. These two roots seem thus to claim a common origin through their individuality, antiquity, and commanding influence in the fulfilment of a common destiny.

WORDS FOR BEING OR EXISTING.

53. Proto-Aryan *as*; Proto-Semitic אש, to be, exist.

For the root *as* cf. Skr. *as*, to be = Gr. ἔς in ἐσ-τί; Lat. *es*, *es-t*; Lith. *es-mi*, I am; Goth. *im*, *is*, *ist*; Engl. *is*. It is generally agreed that it rests upon the root *ás*, to be fixed, to sit (No. 41). — The Semitic root is represented by the Heb. יֵשׁ and אֵשׁ. יֵשׁ and אֵשׁ, there is = the Arab. أَيْسَ; Syr. ܐܺܝܬ; Assyr. *is-u*. The י in Heb. יֵשׁ is plainly secondary, אֵשׁ representing the fundamental Semitic sound, which is revealed in all the other forms. With regard to its origin, it should be remarked that several independent observers have already suspected its affinity with the root אש, to be fixed, to remain (No. 41).[1] Is not this remarkable double parallel with Proto-Aryan forms very strong evidence of the identity of the two pairs of roots here involved?

I have thus taken up the predicative roots of the two systems of speech which seem to justify an attempt to identify them. Something should be said now of those nominal forms which show a mutual resemblance. It should be remarked that, as a general thing, such forms cannot furnish nearly such strong evidence of relationship as do the verbal roots. The reason is plain. The general conceptions con-

---

[2] See what is said by Mühlan and Volck in their edition (the eighth) of Gesenius' Heb. Handwörterbuch. Even Gesenius, who wrongly assigned the Heb. יֵשׁ directly to a root ישה, did not fail to perceive the connection with אשש, etc. (Thesaurus, p. 636).

veyed by such predicative roots as we have been discussing are necessarily expressed by a comparatively limited number of words in any language. If in a large number of these the primary forms and notions correspond to a certainty, the proof of ancient unity is overwhelming. But derivatives are numerous, and are based upon secondary applications of the roots, and not only upon their radical meaning. The chances of coincidence are therefore greater in this region. It should be noticed, again, that the chances of one family borrowing from another the names for sensible objects are immeasurably greater than the chances of appropriating signs for fundamental and generic conceptions, just as it is easier to appropriate a formula than a system of thought, or a maxim than an idea. Very much stress should, therefore, not be laid upon most of the examples of homophonous and synonymous words that might easily be brought forward. We shall, however, discuss two or three that seem worthy of special consideration from the character of the notions they express.

Words for Horn.

54. Proto-Aryan *karna*; Proto-Semitic קרן, a horn.

The Indo-European forms are Lat. *corn-u;* Irish, Welsh, and Cornish *corn;* Teutonic *horn-a* (Goth. *haurn;* Engl., etc. *horn*). The Greek may possibly have had the same word; see Curtius, p. 147 (No. 50). In Skr. it is probably represented in *çrn-ga*, horn. There is another Proto-Aryan word for horn, *kar-va* (Fick, I. 58), which seems connected with words for head, such as Skr. *çir-as;* Gr. κάρ-α, etc.; but no satisfactory root has been found. — For Semitic forms cf. Heb. קֶרֶן; Chald. קַרְנָא; Syr. ܩܰܪܢܳܐ; Arab. قَرْن; Eth. ቀርን; Assyr. *karn-u*. No plausible roots can be found for these forms. If *karn-a* and קֶרֶן are not the same, the identity of the forms might be accounted for either on the assumption that the two were developed quite separately from distinct roots, or on the supposition that in very early times one family borrowed the term from the other. Considering the apparent priority of Proto-Aryan related words it would seem as if, on the latter theory, the Semites must have borrowed from the Aryans.[1] Neither of these hypotheses seems probable, but of the two the second is the less improbable.

55. Proto-Aryan *agra*; Proto-Semitic אגר, a field.

For *agra* cf. Skr. *ajra*, a plain, open country; Gr. ἀγρός; Lat. *ager*; Teutonic *akra* A. S. *acer*; Engl. *acre*, cf. Germ. *acker*), tilled land. The Gr. adj. ἄγρ-ιος agrees with the identical Skr. *ajr-ya* in its sense of belonging to the country, rustic, wild. It is a plausible, though not certain, conjecture of Kuhn (Zeitschrift III. 334), who is followed by Pictet (Origines indo-européennes, 2. ed., II. 108), that the word means properly pasture ground, from *ag*, to drive (Lat. *ag-o*; Gr. ἄγ-ω, etc.), or the place to which flocks are driven.[2] But, as Pictet remarks, the use of the Latin and German words shows that it was very early employed to denote cultivated land. — The Semitic term is found in Assyr. *agar*, a field,[3] in Eth. ሀገር, (1) cultivated, inhabited land, a region, (2) a village, (3) a town or city.[4] In the Himyaritic dialect of Arabic هَجَر means a district, a town. The Ethiopic form appears in Amharic as ሀገር, but this is probably a degeneration.[5] These forms are not susceptible of explanation from any Semitic source. The same alternatives are pre-

[1] Prof. Sayce says, in arguing against Aryo-Semitic relationship (Assyrian Grammar for comparative purposes, p. 14): "Words like קֶרֶן compared with κέρ-ας are borrowed." This implies the belief that such resemblances are not due to mere chance or "onomatopoeia." If they are not borrowed, therefore, they must point to a primary identity. *A fortiori*, then, the conceptual roots compared above, which cannot have been borrowed, point to an ancient oneness of origin. But who would compare directly קֶרֶן with the simpler κέρ-ας?

[2] Cf. Heb. מִדְבָּר, wilderness, from דבר, to drive, and the hometymous Syriac and Ethiopic words (see Gesenius, Thesaurus, p. 318).

[3] For examples of this word, see Norris, Assyr. Dict. i. p. 15.

[4] See Dillmann, Lexicon, col. 20.

[5] Ewald (Ausfürhliches hebr. Lehrbuch, 8th ed. p. 402), who is followed by Dillmann (l. c.), combines these words with Heb. אִכָּר, a tiller, husbandman, and its hometyma in Syriac and Arabic, at the same time connecting all of them with Lat. *ager*, etc. But אִכָּר is probably from אכר, to dig, found in conj. v. in Arabic.

sented as in No. 54. In the present case the chances of the words being borrowed seem very slight, and the chances of fortuitous coincidence no stronger.

WORDS FOR WINE.

56. ? Proto-Aryan *vain;* Proto-Semitic יַיִן, wine.

Leading etymologists are at variance upon all possible questions connected with this most common Indo-European word for wine. The ascertainable forms are Gr. οἶν-ος; Lat. *vîn-um*, anciently *vain-om;* Goth. *vein;* Armenian *gin-i*, for *gwin-i* (= Georgian *gwin-o*), for *win-i*. Similar words in the Keltic seem to have been borrowed from the Latin. For a full discussion of the possible origin, as well as the history, of these words the reader is referred to Pictet.[1] It is difficult to find a suitable etymology in the Indo-European family, though several notable attempts have been made. — The Semitic forms are Heb. יַיִן, for יֵין, wine; Arab. وَيْن, dark-colored grapes; Eth. ⲰⲠⲎ, wine and a vineyard. No satisfactory etymon has been found for these words. It should be remarked that some eminent Indo-European etymologists, after Friedrich Müller, hold to the Semitic origin of the non-Semitic forms. It is probable that both the primitive Semites and primitive Aryans cultivated or were acquainted with the grape-vine. The evidence for the theory of the ancient identity of the terms involved is of the same general character as that adducible for Nos. 54 and 55, though borrowing on one side or other is perhaps more probable in the present instance.

Although many other cases more or less plausible could be cited, these are the only nouns which seem worthy of serious discussion in a treatise like the present. I think they are worthy of attention from impartial students; the agreement between the first two especially seems hard to account for on any other theory than that of oneness in origin.

Another class of words should be mentioned, though not

---

[1] Op. cit. ii. p. 311 ff.; cf. Hintner in Fick's Vergl. Wörterbuch, ii. 795.

168   RELATIONS OF THE ARYAN AND SEMITIC LANGUAGES.

discussed. These are pronominal and demonstrative roots which are surprisingly alike in the two systems. But for two reasons the treatment of them here would be unprofitable: (1) In most cases only a single consonant is found in each one of a pair of similar roots, and the identification is not so conclusive as when two or three consonants are the same. At all events, such combinations would meet with that objection. (2) Such roots are found to be (though in less measure) alike in most of the languages of the world; and it is easy to put aside all these resemblances on the assumption that demonstrative roots, being interjectional in their character, are apt to be alike everywhere, since men, in a state of nature, are held to express similar feelings by similar sounds.

The following table will exhibit in one view the comparable forms which have just been expounded. Some of the forms have a twofold representation which is not exhibited here in every case.

	Proto-Aryan.	Proto-Semitic.			Proto-Aryan.	Proto-Semitic.	
1.	ku	קי	} to burn.	21.	mar	מר	} to rub, or bruise.
2.	kad	קד		22.	mark	מרק	
3.	kar	קל		23.	marg	מרג	
4. ?	us	אש		24.	mard	מרד	
5.	bha	בה	} to shine.	25.	mars	מרש	
6.	bhar	בר		26.	gam	גם	to unite.
7.	bhark	ברק		27.	tan	תן	} to stretch, extend.
8.	bharg	ברג		28.	nat	נט	
9.	bhas	בש		29.	mad	מד	
10.	ark	רק		30.	rak	רך	
11.	bhar	בר	} to cut or separate.	31.	rak	רך	to arrange.
12.	bhid	בר		32.	kap	כף	} to bend.
13.	pat	פת		33.	kmar	קמר	
14.	park	פרק		34.	ak	עק	
15.	kar	כר		35.	sad	צד	} to go.
16.	kart	כרת		36.	sar	שר	
17.	karp	קרף		37.	ragh	רג	to move quickly.
18.	kars	קרש					
19.	sak	שך		38.	di	דא	to fly.
20.	tak	תך					

RELATIONS OF THE ARYAN AND SEMITIC LANGUAGES. 169

	Proto-Aryan.	Proto-Semitic.			Proto-Aryan.	Proto-Semitic.	
39.	tal	חל	to raise, weigh.	48.	? smar	סמר	to pierce.
				49.	sik	שׁק	to moisten.
40.	sad	סר	} to sit.	50.	ḳar	קר	to be cold.
41.	as	אש		51.	man	מן	to think.
42.	man	מן	to be fixed.	52.	vid	ור	to know.
43.	klu	כלא	to shut.	53.	as	אש	to be.
44.	var	ור	to keep off.				
45.	sar	סר	to bind.	54.	ḳarna	קרן	horn.
46.	mak	מך	to press.	55.	agra	אגר	field.
47.	grap glup	גלף	to carve.	56.	? vain	וין	wine.

With regard to these forms, taken in connection with the ideas they express, it is necessary to make some closing remarks:

(1) It should be observed that no form has been admitted against which the objection might fairly be made that it is onomatopoetic in its origin. The list might have been largely increased if such terms had been included.[1] On the other hand, it is impossible, in the case of most of the terms compared, to see how onomatopoeia could have had to do with their origin. The only ones in which this might be suspected are those which express the ideas of cutting or separating and rubbing or bruising. But these notions might be expressed in a hundred different ways; and here the coincidences are so numerous and striking, in both primary and secondary forms, that we must, in reason, either maintain that the onomatopoeia acted in primitive Aryo-Semitic speech, or reject that theory altogether for those classes of roots.

(2) The close phonetic correspondence between the forms compared should be well considered. If it is admitted, as I think it will be, that in these discussions there has been no straining after an imaginary identity of primary meaning

[1] It is to be noted, however, that ideas which are usually held to be expressed most frequently by onomatopoeia are rarely conveyed by similar terms in the two systems of speech. For example, no two terms for breathing are alike, and only one pair of words for calling resemble one another. The onomatopoetic theory is a very easy one to employ, but it is apt to be overworked.

170   RELATIONS OF THE ARYAN AND SEMITIC LANGUAGES.

in the roots and no false phonologizing in the harmonizing of the forms, the results are well worth serious attention from this standpoint. The main fact in the question is simply this: leaving out the cases in which an interrogative mark has been used, we have over fifty pairs of roots which agree exactly in their primary notions and ultimate forms. The value of this fact, as bearing upon the issue involved, may be estimated from the attempt to conceive what the chances would be against such an agreement, if the two linguistic systems did not spring from a common source. That two peoples, not having a common origin or a common early history, should have separately framed a primitive speech from precisely the same elements would seem to be a phonological and psychological miracle after which such difficulties as are presented by the confusion of Babel would become problems only fit for the kindergarten. The chances would have been just as good for a merely partial agreement in any one of an infinite variety of ways. In bi-consonantal forms the first radical and the second in each pair might have been the same and the other two have differed from one another by the whole range of phonetic expression. Or in the dissimilar letters the divergence might have been slight, involving only cases of possible sound-shifting.[1] Of the tri-consonantal roots, of which a goodly number have been cited, a much more various and bewildering series of combinations than even these might have been presented, if the theory of a chance coincidence were valid. And the proved conditions of the question must shut us up to that theory of a purely fortuitous resemblance, unless we assume that the two systems were originally one.

(3) The ideas which are found to be expressed by the

[1] In a few cases, but only in a very few, there are bye-forms in one family or the other, which differ from the forms above compared, by merely this slight measure. The Proto-Aryan root *rag*, to extend, along with the form *rak̬*, has been already alluded to (No. 30). In Proto-Semitic, the only ones are פר and בת, to separate, along with בר, בר, and פת (Nos. 11, 12, 13); מט, to extend, along with מר (No. 29); דל, to raise, along with תל (No. 39), and perhaps בב, to be round, along with קפ, to bend (No. 32).

same forms in the two systems are just those which we should naturally expect to have been employed by a primitive people. The notions are simple and primary. The action of the forces of nature; the most spontaneous works and ways of men and animals; the efforts and movements required in the most essential acts and arts of life, are what we find represented in this brief, but rich vocabulary. There are only three ideas expressed here which do not relate to the world of sense; but these are the most essential of all metaphysical conceptions: to think, to know, to be. Only one term is absent which we might seem to have a right to expect: there is no word in our list relating to human speech. But even this accords with what our observation of language would lead us to look for. Words for speaking are notoriously different, for example, in the different branches of the Indo-European family. They are mostly secondary and originally figurative.[1] The same remark holds equally good of such terms within the Semitic family.[2]

From all that has been said it seems to be a just and necessary conclusion that the primitive Aryans and primitive Semites possessed in common a good working vocabulary.

[1] Proto-Aryan words for speaking are but few, and most of them are but sparsely represented. Only one, the root *vak* has been at all persistent. Pictet has no treatment of this subject in his "Origines indo-européennes."

[2] In fact, it is doubtful whether any Proto-Semitic word for speaking has survived.

INDEXES.

[Compare the Table of Contents and the List of Comparable Roots, pp. 168, 169. The large figures refer to the special comparisons].

I. PROTO-ARYAN.

	PAGE		PAGE
'*ak* ('*ank*), to bend, curve,	148	*ḳi*, to lie,	114
'*agra*, field,	166	*ḳu* (*ḳav*), to burn,	123
'*agh* ('*angh*), to press,	84	*ḳvid*, to be white,	123
'*ad*, to eat,	115		
'*ark* (*rak*), to shine,	127	*ga*, to beget,	86
'*arg* (*rag*), to shine,	83, 87, 127	*ga* (*gam*), to go,	87
'*arbh*, to obtain,	83	*gan*, to know,	85
'*as*, to throw,	119	*gan*, to beget,	86
'*as* (*ás*), to sit, remain,	153	*gam*, to unite,	140
'*as*, to be,	164	*gna*, to know,	85
		grap, to carve, grave,	158
'*i*, to go,	114	*grup*, to curve,	158
'*is*, to throw,	119		
		ghar, to seize,	87
ug (*vag*), to grow,	87	*gharbh*, to seize,	87
us (*vas*), to burn,	82, 124		
		tak, to cut,	135
kad (*kand*), to burn,	123	*taks*, to hew,	136
kap, to bend, curve,	147	*tan* (*ta*), to stretch,	83, 86, 89, 141
kar, to make,	86	*tar*, to cross over,	87
kar, to divide,	86, 131	*tal*, to raise, weigh,	151
kart, to cleave,	86, 115, 132		
karp (*kalp*), to procure,	86	*da*, to give,	114
karp, to cut off,	133	*da*, to bind,	87, 88
kars, to tear apart,	133	*da*, to divide,	82, 85, 87
ku, to conceal,	86	*daḳ*, to bite,	85
kudh, to conceal,	86	*daḳ*, to show,	82
kmar, to bend,	147	*dap*, to divide,	86
klu, to shut,	115, 154	*dam*, to bind, tame,	87, 88
		dar, to see,	85
ḳar (*ḳal*), to heat, cook,	124	*dar*, to burst,	87
ḳarna, horn,	165	*darḳ*, to see,	85
ḳav, to burn,	123	*di*, to divide,	82

INDEX I.

di, to hasten,	82, 150	mad, to measure,	86, 143
di, to shine,	82, 119	man, to measure, think,	86, 88, 161
dik, to show,	82	man, to remain, be fixed,	153
div, to shine,	83, 119	mand, to decorate,	119
du, to burn,	83, 119	mar, to rub, crush,	82, 86, 90, 136
dra (dram), to run,	87, 115	mark, to touch, stroke,	85, 90, 137
		marg, to stroke, wipe,	85, 90, 137
dhar, to hold firm,	87	mard, to crush,	86, 90, 115, 138
dharg, to drag,	86	mardh, to relax,	.90
dhars, to be bold,	87	mars, to oppress, obstruct,	139
dhi, to see,	85	mud, to be lively,	83, 119, 120
dhya, to see,	85	mund, to decorate,	119
		mna, to remember,	88
nat (nit), to stretch, incline,	142		
nu, to float,	83, 88	yag, to worship,	82
		yu, to join,	82, 85
pa, to drink,	82, 119	yug, to join,	85
pa, to protect,	86		
pa, to obtain,	86	ra (ram), to enjoy,	87
pat, to rule,	86	rak, to shine,	127
pat, to attain,	86	rak, to dispose, arrange,	146
pat, to separate, open,	130	rak, to extend,	145
park, to cleave,	131	rag, to color,	83, 87, 127
pi, to drink,	82, 119	râg, to shine,	127
prak, to ask,	115	ragh, to move quickly,	150
prat, to spread,	115	ri, to anoint,	86
pri, to love,	82, 115	rip, to anoint,	86
pru (plu), to swim,	115	ru (lu), to separate,	82
bha, to shine,	85, 87, 92, 125	vain (?) wine,	167
bhag, to divide, share,	83, 129	vaks, to grow,	87
bhad, to cleave,	119	vag (ug), to increase,	87
bhar, to divide,	92, 129	var, to guard against,	155
bhar, to bear,	82	vas (us), to burn,	82
bhar, to shine,	85, 92, 125	vid, to know,	82, 162
bhark, to shine,	85, 126		
bharg, to shine,	85, 87, 92, 115, 126	sa, to sit,	86
bharg, to break,	92	sak, to cut,	135
bhas, to shine,	87, 127	sak, to moisten,	160
bhid, to split,	119, 129	sad, to sit,	86, 152
bhu, to be,	82	sad, to go,	149
bhug, to share, enjoy,	83, 119	sar, to bind,	156
		sar, to go,	86, 149
ma, to diminish,	82	sarp, to creep,	86
ma, to measure,	86, 143, 161	si, to bind,	119, 120
mak, to press,	157	sik, to moisten, pour out,	160
mak, to extend,	144	siv, to sew,	83
mag, to extend,	144	su, to sew,	83, 119, 120
magh, to extend,	144	ska, to cut,	135
mad, to be excited,	83, 119, 120	ska, to cover,	119

skad, to split,	119	*star*, to place firmly,		87
skar, to divide,	86	*snu*, to float,		83, 88
skid, to split,	119	*spak̲*, to see,		82
sku, to conceal,	86, 119	*spargh*, to strive after,		115
sta, to stand,	87	*smar* (?) to pierce, infix,		159
stan, to sound,	83, 89	*smard* to gnaw at,		115
stabh, to support,	87	*svad*, to taste,		88

II. PROTO-SEMITIC.

אבד *'-b-d*, to be separated, to be lost,	99, 115	ברך *b-r-k*, to kneel, bless,		115
אגד *'-g-d*, to bind,	109	ברק *b-r-k̲*, to lighten,		126
אגר *'agar-u*, a field,	166	בשל *b-s-l*, to cook,		127
איל *'-(w)-l*, to be strong,	115	בשר *b-s-r*, to be joyful,		127
אכף *'-k-p*, to bend,	99	בת *b-t*, to separate,		130
אל *'il-u*, God,	107	גבן *g-b-n*, to be curved (?),		109
אלה *'ilah-u*, God,	107	גד *g-d*, to cut,		110
אמן *'-m-n*, to remain, be firm,	100, 154	גדל *g-d-l*, to twist together, make great,		109
אסף *'-s′-p*, to accumulate,	99	גדע *g-d-ʿ*, to hew off,		110
אסר *'-s′-r*, to bind,	99, 157	גיר *g-(w)-r*, to turn aside, sojourn,		103
ארך *'-r-k*, to stretch out,	101, 146	גיד *g-(y)-d*, to bind,		109
אש *'-s*, to be placed, remain,	153	גלב *g-l-b*, to drag off,		107
אש *'-s*, to be,	164	גלד *g-l-d*, to tear off,		107
אש *'is-u*, fire,	124	גלו *g-l-w*, to lay bare,	107,	108
אשר *'-s-r*, to go right,	100	גלח *g-l-ḥ*, to smooth off,	107,	108
		גלף *g-l-p*, to carve, grave,		158
באר *b-'-r*, to dig,	102, 129	גם *g-m*, to bring together,		140
בב *bāb-u*, a gate,	114	גמר *g-m-r*, to complete,		141
בד *b-d*, to cut off,	99, 105, 115, 130	גר *g-r*, to drag, scrape, roll,	101, 106 109,	110
בחר *b-h-r*, to shine,	125			
בוא *b-(w)-'*, to go in,	114, 115	גרב *g-r-b*, to be scabby,		106
בוץ *b-(w)-ṣ*, to be white,	127	גרל *g-r-l*, to drag off,		109
בור *b-(w)-r*, to explore,	129	גרן *gurn-u*, threshing-floor,		109
בל *b-l*, to be confused,	107	גרף *g-r-p*, sweep away,		110
בלג *b-l-g*, to be bright,	126			
בלח *b-l-ḥ*, to be abashed,	107	דא *d-'*, to move swiftly, fly,		151
בער *b-ʿ-d*, to be separated,	105, 130	דחר *d-h-r*, to revolve,		103
בער *b-ʿ-r*, to cut off, consume,	129	דור *d-(w)-r*, to turn round,		103
בר *b-r*, to cut, divide,	99, 102, 105, 108, 129	די *d-y*, to fly,		151
ברא *b-r-'*, to hew out, create,	106, 129	דל *d-l*, to hang loose,	100,	108
ברז *b-r-z*, to pierce,	108, 129	דלו *d-l-w*, to suspend,	108,	115
ברזל (פרזל) *barzil-u (parzil-u)*, iron,	108, 116, 129			
ברח *b-r-ḥ*, to pass through,	108, 129	דר *d-r*, to move round,	103,	109
ברי *b-r-y*, to cut,	129	דרג *d-r-g*, to go by steps,	107,	109
		דרך *d-r-k*, to tread,	107,	109

INDEX II. 175

חבר h-b-r, to divide up,	99, 129
הלך h-l-k, to go away,	99
חרם h-r-m, to be high,	99
ובל w-b-l, to flow,	102
ודי w-d-y (in caus. forms), to make known,	163
וירע v-d-', to know,	163
ויין wain-u, wine,	167
ובל w-k-l, to contain,	100, 115
וסד v-s'-d, to set, place,	152
ורא v-r-', to guard against, fear,	156
ורד v-r-d, to go down,	99
וירע v-r-', to fear,	156
ורק w-r-k, to be green or yellow,	128
ורק w-r-k, to be behind,	146
ותן w-t-n, to be perpetual,	142
זרו z-r-w, to scatter,	110
זרע z-r-', to sow,	110
חדל h-d-l, to let go,	100
חט h-t, to cut,	106
חטב h-t-b, to hew wood,	106
חם h-m, to be warm,	107
חמד h-m-d, to be ardent,	107
חנק h-n-k, to press tight	100
חר h-r, to cut open,	108
חרט h-r-t, to grave,	108
חריץ h-r-s, to cut open,	134
חרש h-r-s, to plough,	134
חתם h-t-m, to close, seal,	100
טול t-(w)-l, to be long,	101
יום yum-u, day,	103
ים yam-u, sea,	103
ימן y-m-n, to be strong (?),	100
יצע y-s-', to place,	110
יקד y-k-d, to burn,	124
יקץ y-k-s, to awake,	100
ישר y-s-r, to be right,	100, 115
כב k-b, to bend,	102
כוי k-w-y, to burn,	123
כול k-(w)-l, to contain,	144
כון k-(w)-n, to be fixed,	102, 115
כיר k-(w)-r, to dig,	132
כל k-l, to enclose,	100, 155
כלא k-l-', to shut,	106, 115, 155

כן k-n, to be fixed,	102
כף k-p, to bend,	99, 147
כרו k-r-w, to pierce, dig,	132
כרת k-r-t, to cut off,	132
לאך l-'-k, to send,	99
מאד m-'-d, to be large,	102, 145
מאי m-'-y, to extend,	145
מאס m-'-s', to flow,	102
מד m-d, to extend,	102, 145
מהר m-h-r, to sell,	104
מון m-(w)-n, to think, conceive,	162
מור m-(w)-r, to exchange,	104
מחר m-h-r, to exchange (?),	104
מטל m-t-l, to extend,	101
מך m-k, to press down,	157
מלא m-l-', to fill,	106
מני m-n-y, to measure out,	162
מס m-s', to be liquid,	102
מעך m-'-k, to press,	158
מרג m-r-g, to rub hard, to press,	137
מרד m-r-d, to bruise,	138
מרח m-r-h, to rub,	137
מרי m-r-y, to rub against,	137
מרץ m-r-s, to press upon,	139
מרק m-r-k, to rub off,	137
נגר n-g-r, to move along,	101
נד n-d, to move violently,	103
נהר n-h-r, to shine forth,	103
נוד n-(w)-d, to flee,	103
נור n-(w)-r, to shine,	103
נטו n-t-w, to stretch forwards,	143
נטע n-t-', to set in,	110
נך n-k, to strike,	109
נכי n-k-y, to smite,	108
נסך n-s'-k, to weave together,	101
נק n-k, to strike apart,	109
נקי n-k-y, to be separate, pure,	109, 115
נתן n-t-n, to give,	101, 142
נתע n-t-', to stretch forwards,	143
סב s'-b, to turn round,	103
סבע s'ab-'-u, seven,	110
סד s'-d, to set down,	153
סחר s'-h-r, to be round,	104
סור s'-(w)-r, to turn aside,	104
סחר s'-h-r, to traverse,	104
סך s'-k, to weave, cover,	101

INDEX II.

סף s´-p, to scrape,	99	צער ṣ-'-r, to be small,	105
סר s´-r, to bind,	99	צר ṣ-r, to bind, press together, 105, 157

ער '-d, to arrange, number,	103	קדח ḳ-d-ḥ, to kindle,	124
עור '-(w)-d, to repeat,	103	קדש ḳ-d-s, to be pure, sacred,	115
עוק '-(w)-ḳ, to restrain,	148	קום ḳ-(w)-m, to stand up,	104
עור '-(w)-r, to be bare,	109	קור ḳ-(w)-r, to dig or cut out,	132
עז '-z, to be strong,	115	קין ḳ-(y)-n, to fashion,	105
ענק '-n-ḳ, to put around the neck, (denom.),	100	קלו ḳ-l-w, to roast, burn,	124
		קלף ḳ-l-p, to tear off,	133
עצו '-ṣ-w, to be firm,	109	קמר ḳ-m-r, to make round,	148
עצם '-ṣ-m, to be strong, great,	109	קן ḳ-n, to be fixed, 102, 105, 108
עקב '-ḳ-b, to arch,	148	קנא ḳ-n-', to be moved with passion, 106
עקל '-ḳ-l, to bind, twist,	148	קני ḳ-n-y, to found, acquire,	108
עקם '-ḳ-m, to twist, restrain,	148	קר ḳ-r, to cut, dig, 101, 132
עקץ '-ḳ-ṣ, to twist,	148	קר ḳ-r, to be cold,	161
עקר '-ḳ-r, to cut out,	101	קרט ḳ-r-ṭ, to cut up, 132, 135
עקש '-ḳ-s, to twist,	148	קרן ḳarn-u, horn,	165
ערו '-r-w, to be bare,	109	קרץ ḳ-r-ṣ, to cut off,	134
ערם '-r-m, to be bare,	109	קרש ḳ-r-s, to cut off,	134
ערך '-r-k, to arrange,	101, 147		
עתד '-t-d, to prepare,	106	ראי r-'-y, to see,	115
		רג r-g, to move quickly,	150
פוח p-(w)-ḥ, to spread out,	130	רגז r-g-z, to tremble,	150
פטר p-ṭ-r, to open,	111, 130	רגל r-g-l, to move about, run,	150
פל p-l, to cleave,	107	רד r-d, to move, push,	100
פלג p-l-g, to divide,	107		
פלט p-l-ṭ, to break away,	108	שבל s-b-l, to flow,	102
פלק p-l-ḳ, to cleave,	131	שבע s-b-', to be full,	110
פר p-r, to cleave, 107, 108, 109, 111	שוב s-(w)-b, to return,	103
פרד p-r-d, to separate,	107	שור s-(w)-r, to move quickly,	149
פרץ p-r-z, to branch out,	108	שית s-(y)-t, to lay down,	105
פרך p-r-k, to crush,	109, 131	שך s-k, to cut, pierce,	135
פרס p-r-s', to break up,	110	שכב s-k-b, to lie,	102
פרץ p-r-ṣ, to break open,	111	שכן s-k-n, to establish,	102
פרק p-r-ḳ, to separate,	131	שלט s-l-ṭ, to be strong, rule,	115
פרש p-r-s, to disperse,	111, 116	שמר s-m-r, to pierce, infix,	160
פרשד p-r-s-d, to spread out,	116	שנק s-n-ḳ, to strangle,	100
פת p-t, to break off,	130	שק s-ḳ, to cleave,	135
פתח p-t-ḥ, to open,	130	שקי s-ḳ-y, to moisten, pour out,	160
		שר s-r, to saw,	108
צד ṣ-d, to go aside,	149	שרט s-r-ṭ, to cut open,	108
צדק ṣ-d-ḳ, to go right,	149	שרע s-r-', to glide along,	150
ציד ṣ-(w)-d, to go after, hunt,	149	שת s-t, to lay,	105
צלא ṣ-l-', to incline,	107		
צלב ṣ-l-b, to hang up,	106	תך t-k, to cut into,	136
צם ṣ-m, to shut up,	111	תל t-l, to raise, suspend,	151
צמא ṣ-m-', to thirst,	106	תלו t-l-w, to hang, adhere to,	152
צמת ṣ-m-t, to be silent,	111	תן t-n, to stretch, 101, 141
צער ṣ-'-d, to go up or down,	149	תקן t-ḳ-n, to be straight,	102

www.ingramcontent.com/pod-product-compliance
Lightning Source LLC
Chambersburg PA
CBHW070331230426
43663CB00011B/2274